THE BEST OF
PETER HOWARD

THE BEST OF PETER HOWARD

NEW
HOLLAND

For the farmers, graziers, fishermen and all associated with the outstanding foods and wines of this amazing country, Australia – thanks!

CONTENTS

INTRODUCTION

There can be no doubt that when you are about to have a collection of recipes assembled under the title of "The Best Of..." you know you have been around for while. Indeed I am lucky to be in my sixties and I do ponder where the years have gone. At this age, who doesn't?

With so much of my life having been spent in a marvellous and fulfilling career that was in the public eye, there is plenty to reflect on. I was given gifts which gave me a career as a multimedia chef, a teacher, a public stomach, a representative of Australia and so much more.

My 33-year career as a food and wine journalist plus cookbook author, is a monumental achievement. I say that with great humility as I came from a small country town in Queensland and never thought I would be on stages around the world and featuring on a TV show with an audience of around 23 million viewers. That is one appearance I will not forget – the NBC Today Show had a barbecue in Rockerfeller Plaza on a brilliant Sunday morning in sparkling New York City. That is now many years ago now, in the late 1990s.

The centre of attention on that day was my first barbeque book with New Holland and my first book to be sold into the USA and to go international. What did I cook for that event? Australian lamb, what else! That book also made it possible for me to travel to London and appear on Good Morning Britain.

I have thousands of different and memorable experiences that I could recall, but the question that I've been asked the most is: "How did you start? Bet your mum taught all you know!"

My mother was a great cook and very happy to impart her knowledge later in life. However, when I was in my formative years, she had me, my five siblings, my dad and her father to feed. Yes, a large household of nine hungry mouths. She always served us two courses for our main meal – normally dinner. In those frantic days she did not have time to begin teaching me "...now you must carefully add this and stir it clockwise..."

However, later in life she showed me how to make delicious things they don't teach you at catering school. Her lemon butter and mixed citrus marmalade are particularly special to me. Thanks Mum!

What my parents did teach me and my siblings was to respect and love food. I say respect in that I was born just after the Second World War (1947) when food was not that abundant. We ate what was put in front of us and were grateful for it – luckily it was well cooked by a mother who loved her family and her culinary output. We respected the hard work that went into our meals, not only by our mother but also the farmers, many of whom were our relatives in the region.

In writing this introduction it is easy to get carried away with what one has done. Ultimately, it is imperative to acknowledge who the real stars are in a career such as mine. While I may have been given a talent to cook, it was enhanced by dedicated teachers and mentors like Graham Latham OAM. The farmers of this great country of Australia also underpin everything I have ever done.

Where would any of us be without our primary producers, who I think are the best in the world. In the couple of decades that I worked at the RAS in the annual Royal Easter Show I met so many of them. I used their produce and products for every meal. These products were my conduit to TV shows and demonstration cooking in so many places in Australia and around the world. Their produce also featured in all my cookbooks – I have written nearly 20 since my first one was released in 1983. And how many column inches have I notched up writing about the output of our dedicated farmers? I would not even try to consider. I did once estimate that during my 16 years with the Channel 9 Network I made over 1000 appearances. Whatever the highlights and the memories of my career, the farmers were always there and I owe so much to them for their enormous hard work. Thanks guys.

When you start to acknowledge people who were instrumental in your career, you inevitably miss out someone who should have been mentioned – apologies if you are one of those forgotten people.

New Holland Publishers must always be acknowledged as they have given me a platform for my books for many, many years. They are professional, patient, inspiring, knowledgeable and supportive.

Many Australian stars have been supportive over the years and people like Mike Carlton, Ray Martin, Steve Liebmann, Liz Hayes, Ben Ulm, David Peters, Gloria Zimmerebner and Doreen Peacock were invaluable. Lyndey Milan OAM and Doug Crosby OAM are to be listed too. These are a few of the people who have made my career a memorable and wonderful journey. My private life has been equally exciting and rewarding, mostly because of what I did as a living. Many thanks to my partner, Gregor Eastham, for his constant support.

However, without you – my readers and supporters – I would not have had a career at all. While I did officially stop working in 2010, it is not possible to stop loving food and wine in this great country of ours. What a fantastic food industry we have and what a country we live in – Australia!

Once again, sincere thanks to New Holland. I hope you use and enjoy this book.

BASICS

BARBECUE GARLIC DRESSING

→ INGREDIENTS

- 30 g (1 oz) cloves garlic, cut in half
- 250 ml (8 fl oz) light olive oil
- ½ teaspoon salt
- ¼ teaspoon freshly ground black pepper
- 1 teaspoon white sugar
- 2 tablespoons Spanish sherry vinegar

→ METHOD

Spray the flat plate with oil and cook garlic for four minutes, turning it regularly to allow it to brown lightly. Lift from the barbecue.

Return to the kitchen and process garlic with oil, salt, pepper and sugar in a food processor or blender until smooth and light cream in colour.

With motor running, add vinegar through the feed chute and, when combined, switch off and pour this rich dressing into a screw top jar. Keep refrigerated in fridge for up to 2 weeks.

BASIC HANDMADE MAYONNAISE

You can make this unique sauce in a processor or blender, but I always do it by hand. Something seems to happen when it's mixed with a balloon whisk that gives it just a little extra magic. Once you've tried this mayonnaise you'll never want to use anything else.

→ INGREDIENTS

- 2 large egg yolks, at room temperature
- ½ teaspoon salt
- pinch white pepper
- ½ teaspoon prepared mustard (smooth Dijon is best)
- 1 teaspoon white vinegar
- 250 ml (8 fl oz) light olive oil

→ METHOD

Place egg yolks, salt, pepper, mustard and vinegar in a clean, warm mixing bowl. Secure the bowl by wrapping a damp tea towel around its base to keep it steady on the bench. Alternatively, ask somebody to hold the bowl in place.

With a clean balloon whisk, whisk these ingredients together until light gold in colour. Whisk in the oil, almost drop by drop until you have added a third. Slowly increase the flow of oil to a thin, steady stream until all oil has been incorporated. Keep refrigerated for up to 6 days.

GARLIC CROUTONS

→ **INGREDIENTS**

- 4 slices day old rye and linseed bread or similar (I use Burgen)
- 1 tablespoon garlic, crushed
- spray vegetable oil

→ **METHOD**

Cut the bread into 2 cm squares. Place into a non-stick frying pan, add the garlic and spray with oil. Put on a medium heat and toss to colour and crisp. You need to keep the croutons moving so the garlic doesn't discolour.

Tip onto a kitchen towel-lined plate and cool. Use when ready.

These are flavour bombs with that added crunch for salad and soups. They store well in an airtight container and you'll be surprised where you will find a use for them. You will use them all at once for 4 serves. If you make them a little bigger, you can use them as a small biscuit for dips.

BLUE CHEESE DRESSING

→ INGREDIENTS

- 60 g (2 oz) blue vein cheese, such as Gorgonzola or Milawa blue
- 2 teaspoons white wine vinegar
- 250 ml (8 fl oz) traditional vinaigrette

→ METHOD

Place cheese in a bowl and mash to a paste with vinegar. When fully combined, stir in vinaigrette.

Pour into a storage container.

Shake dressing well before using.

CHILLI JAM

→ INGREDIENTS

- 60 g (2 oz) large Thai chillies, dried
- 315 g (10 oz) red Thai shallots, fried
- 155 g (5 oz) garlic, fried
- 60 g (2 oz) dried prawns
- 250 g (8 oz) palm sugar
- 125 g (4 oz) tamarind pulp

→ METHOD

Roast the chillies briefly in a dry frying pan. Using a mortar and pestle or food processor, blend all ingredients to a smooth paste. Transfer to a saucepan and bring to the boil over a medium heat. Reduce heat and simmer, stirring constantly as jam cooks for 5 minutes.

Spoon into sterilized jars and cover with lids when cool. It will keep refrigerated for a long time.

NAM JIM DRESSING

→ INGREDIENTS

- 3 cloves garlic, peeled and crushed
- 3 green chillies, seeded and roughly chopped
- 3 coriander roots, washed and trimmed
- 150 ml (5 fl oz) lime juice, freshly squeezed
- 60 ml (2 fl oz) nam pla (fish sauce)
- 30 g (1 oz) caster sugar

→ METHOD

Combine all ingredients and work to a rough paste. Serve immediately.

HOMEMADE BARBECUE SAUCE

→ INGREDIENTS

- 30 g (1 oz) garlic cloves, peeled
- 250 ml (8 fl oz) orange juice
- 250 ml (8 fl oz) tomato juice
- 250 ml (8 fl oz) red wine
- 125 ml (4 fl oz) golden syrup
- 60 ml (2 fl oz) malt vinegar
- 60 g (2 oz) onion, chopped

→ METHOD

Spray the flat plate lightly with oil, and cook garlic for four minutes, turning constantly to brown it lightly.

Remove from heat.

Puree garlic with remaining ingredients in a food processor or blender. Pour into a saucepan and simmer for 15–20 minutes, or until reduced to the consistency of commercial tomato sauce. Keeps for 2 weeks.

LEMON AND MUSTARD BUTTER

→ INGREDIENTS

- 225 g (8 oz) butter, at room temperature
- 1 tablespoon lemon juice, freshly juiced
- 1 tablespoon seeded mustard
- 1 tablespoon parsley, chopped
- 1 teaspoon freshly ground black pepper

→ METHOD

Put all ingredients in a bowl and mix well using either your hands or a wooden spoon. Scrape the mixed butter into a storage container and refrigerate. Alternatively, shape it into a sausage, roll it up in greaseproof paper or plastic wrap and freeze.

GARLIC OIL

→ INGREDIENTS

- 2 large heads of garlic, unpeeled
- 500 ml (16 fl oz) extra virgin olive oil

→ METHOD

Cut garlic heads, crosswise, about a third of the way form the top of each head. Keep the garlic tops for another use.

Spray the flat plate with oil and cook cut garlic heads, cut side down, for 7 minutes. Remove from the heat and put into an airtight storage container. Cover with oil and leave to sit for 2 days before use. If you haven't used the oil within 6 days of preparing it, remove and discard garlic from the oil, return the lid and store oil in a cool, dark place. Keeps for 2 weeks.

PEANUT SAUCE

→ INGREDIENTS

- 155 g (5 oz) peanut butter
- 250 ml (8 fl oz) water
- 1 clove garlic, peeled and crushed
- 2 teaspoons palm sugar
- 1 red chilli, seeded and roughly chopped
- 60 ml (2 fl oz) light soy sauce
- 1 tablespoon lemon juice
- 1 tablespoon fish sauce
- 125 ml (4 fl oz) coconut milk

→ METHOD

Combine peanut butter and water in a saucepan, stirring over moderate heat until well mixed.

Remove from heat and add remaining ingredients.

Return to moderate heat and cook, stirring, for 5–6 minutes, or until a thick paste forms. Keeps in the refrigerator for 3 weeks.

TRADITIONAL VINAIGRETTE

→ INGREDIENTS

- 60 ml (2 fl oz) olive oil
- 1 clove garlic, crushed
- ½ teaspoon dry Dijon mustard
- 1 tablespoon white vinegar
- 1 tablespoon parsley, finely chopped
- ½ teaspoon salt
- ¼ teaspoon white pepper

→ METHOD

Put the oil, garlic and mustard in a large bowl and whisk with a balloon whisk until the mixture is a creamy consistency and light yellow in colour. Whisk in the vinegar and add parsley, salt and pepper. Stir until combined.

The best way to coat salad leaves with vinaigrette is to tumble them in a small amount of dressing. There should never be any dressing left sitting in the bottom of the bowl.

WASABI BUTTER

→ INGREDIENTS

- 250 g (8 oz) unsalted butter, at room temperature
- 1–2 teaspoons Wasabi paste (or to taste)
- 2 tablespoons garlic chives, finely chopped
- 1 tablespoon rice vinegar

→ METHOD

Mash all ingredients together in a bowl until well combined. Roll into a sausage shape in cling wrap or waxed paper and secure by twisting the ends of the cling wrap or waxed paper. Freeze until ready to use.

BASIC INDIAN SPRINKLE

This versatile sprinkle can be used to highlight the flavour of lots of barbecued goodies. I use it on fish, steaks and chicken and love what it does to potatoes and eggplant (aubergine). Keep it handy and you'll come to love it like I do.

→ INGREDIENTS

- 2 tablespoons ground cumin seeds
- 1 tablespoon salt
- ¾ tablespoon ground fennel
- 1 teaspoon garam masala
- ½ teaspoon paprika
- ¼ teaspoon chilli powder

→ METHOD

Mix all the ingredients together. Store in an airtight container and use within 7 days.

BARBECUE TOMATO RELISH

→ INGREDIENTS

- 6 large, semi-ripe tomatoes
- 1 large onion, finely chopped
- 3 garlic cloves, finely chopped
- 2 tablespoons sugar
- 60 ml (2 fl oz) apple juice
- 1 tablespoon mustard powder
- 2 tablespoons curry powder
- 120 ml (4 fl oz) Worchestshire sauce
- 1 tablespoon tamarind pulp
- 1 bay leaf
- 6 whole cloves
- cinnamon curl
- 1 teaspoon salt

→ METHOD

Remove the eyes form the bases of the tomatoes and dice roughly.

Put all ingredients, except salt, into a copper saucepan and simmer until the onion is cooked and the flavours combined, around 10 minutes, stirring constantly.

Add the salt and cook for a further 5–10 minutes, stirring all the time. It is at this time that the relish can stick and burn on the bottom of the pan. Remove from the heat and cool before storing in sterilized airtight containers. Tomato relish keeps for at least 4 weeks in the refrigerator.

GREEN CURRY PASTE

→ INGREDIENTS

- 1 teaspoon cumin seeds
- 2 teaspoons coriander seeds
- 2 green spring onions, trimmed, washed and finely sliced
- 3 cloves garlic, peeled and roughly chopped
- 3 cm (1 in) piece galangal, peeled and roughly chopped
- 1 teaspoon fish sauce
- 6 small red chillies, de-seeded and roughly chopped
- 3 kaffir lime leaves, vein removed and finely chopped
- 1 tablespoon roasted shrimp paste
- 2 tablespoons raw peanuts, roughly chopped

→ METHOD

Dry-fry the cumin and coriander seeds over medium heat for 1 minute or until lightly browned. Cool and then grind into powder using a mortar and pestle or a special spice grinder.

Combine the onions, garlic, galangal and fish sauce in a food processor pound with a mortar and pestle. When a paste begins to form, add the remaining ingredients including the cumin and coriander powder, and work into a paste.

Keep in an airtight container in the refrigerator for up to 2 days.

ROCKET AIOLI

→ INGREDIENTS

- 3 large cloves garlic
- ½ teaspoon sea salt
- 2 egg yolks
- 15 g (½ oz) rocket, blanched

- 250 ml (8 fl oz) pure olive oil
- 1 teaspoon lemon juice

→ METHOD

Place the garlic, salt, egg yolks and rocket into a food processor bowl and chop or process with a chopped blade for 30 seconds.

When the mixture starts to thicken, slowly pour the oil down the feed chute. As it mixed in, you can add the oil a little more quickly until finished.

Stir in the lemon juice just before serving. Aioli may be stored in the refrigerator for no more than 5 days.

CHERMOULA

This delicious spice mix is very versatile. You often see it used with lamb or chicken, and it can also be used for prawns.

→ INGREDIENTS

- 1 medium onion, very finely chopped
- 2 teaspoons fresh coriander leaves, finely chopped
- 2 cloves garlic, minced
- 4 teaspoons ground cumin seeds
- 2 teaspoons mild paprika
- 1 teaspoon powdered turmeric
- ¼ teaspoon cayenne pepper
- ¼ teaspoon each of sea salt and ground black pepper

→ METHOD

Mix all the ingredients together and use as required. While chermoula keeps in the refrigerator for up to a week, the idea with aromatic mixes is to use them as soon as they are made.

ENTREES

THAI CHICKEN CAKES
MAKES 15–20

→ INGREDIENTS

- 500 g (16 oz) chicken thigh fillets
- 1 red capsicum (pepper), finely chopped
- 2 red chillies, chopped
- 2 cloves garlic, chopped
- 1 tablespoons ginger, minced
- 1 stalk of lemongrass, tender part only, chopped
- 2 lime kaffir leaves, ribs removed and shredded

- 1 tablespoon fish sauce
- 120 ml (4 fl oz) coconut milk
- 1 whole egg
- 125 g (4 oz) beans or snake beans, cut into 3 mm (0.1 in) slices
- 60 g (2 oz) fresh breadcrumbs
- Vegetable/peanut oil
- Sweet chilli dipping sauce

→ METHOD

Cut chicken thigh fillets into small pieces.

Combine capsicum, chillies, garlic, ginger, lemon grass, Kaffir leaves and fish sauce into a food processor and blend to a smooth paste. Add chicken pieces, coconut milk and egg and blend well. Place mixture in a bowl and add sliced beans. Chill for at least 1 hour and then stir in the breadcrumbs (you may not need them all but you need a firm dough – not sloppy) to take up some of the excess moisture.

Pour oil onto a medium hot plate and shape a half tablespoon of the chicken mixture into a small cake as you place it on the barbie – do not overload as the chicken cakes cook quickly. I normally do six at a time. Ensure the plate is oiled where you are going to turn the half cooked cakes, then flip them over to cook through. Drain on plate lined with kitchen paper and keep warm. Repeat until all the mixture has gone.

Serve on a platter with the dipping sauce on the side.

SEMILLON SAUVIGNON BLANC OYSTERS

`SERVES 4`

This wine sauce is similar to a 'beurre blanc' and you can use it over barbecued white fish. You can add citrus to it to make it appropriate to the occasion.

→ INGREDIENTS

- 48 freshly shucked small Pacific oysters, on the shell
- 250 ml (8 fl oz) Semillon Sauvignon Blanc wine
- 2 tablespoons chives, chopped
- 1 teaspoon pink peppercorns, rinsed and roughly crushed
- 250g (9oz) salted butter, in cubes

→ METHOD

Check the oysters are grit free – try not to rinse under running water as you lose that lovely saltwater flavour of freshly shucked oysters.

Boil the wine and simmer for 2 minutes; add the chives and peppercorns and simmer for a minute. Remove from the heat and swirl in the butter to melt and add the peppercorns – combine well.

Put the oysters, shell-side down, onto the open grill about eight at a time – spoon over some of the sauce. When the liquid is bubbling, the oysters are ready to serve.

Lift from the barbecue and onto either heaped rock salt on a platter to keep the oysters upright or on finely shredded outer lettuce leaves for the purpose. Leave to cool so they can be picked up and slipped out of the shell and into your mouth around the barbie.

ANGELS ON HORSEBACK
SERVES 4

→ INGREDIENTS

- 16 large oysters out of shell
- 16 pieces of bacon, rindless, 8 cm long x 3 cm wide (3 in x 1 in)
- Toothpicks
- Worcestershire sauce

→ METHOD

Wrap each oyster in a piece of bacon and secure with a toothpick.

Spray a hot plate with a little oil and cook the angels at high temperature until bacon is crisp. Brush a little Worcestershire sauce onto the oysters as they cook.

Serve the angels on suitable plate with a little Worcestershire sauce on the side – these are great served around the barbie as guests arrive.

ASIAN-FLAVOURED SEA SCALLOPS
SERVES 4

→ INGREDIENTS

- 20 scallops on shell
- Spray vegetable oil
- 3 tablespoons green spring onions, minced
- 1 tablespoon thick soy sauce (Kepak Manis)
- 1 teaspoon green ginger, finely minced
- 1 teaspoon lemongrass, white only, minced
- 1 tablespoon lime juice
- 1 small green chilli, seeds removed and minced
- ½ tablespoon water

→ METHOD

Check each scallop to see it is clean and grit free – lift each scallop and give the shell a film of oil with the spray and return the scallop. Repeat for all the scallops and refrigerate until ready to cook.

Mix the remaining ingredients and spoon a little over each scallop on the shell.

Lift onto medium hot grillcook a few at a time as they cook quickly. Turn the scallops carefully if you can on the grill, otherwise lift from grill and turn over. Spoon over a little more sauce, cook further and serve when all are done to your liking.

BABA GANOUSH
MAKES 600 G (21 OZ)

If you use pita bread, it is served either cut into triangles or whole so pieces can be ripped from it. You can also serve the spread on a flat plate with olive oil drizzled over the top in which case you drag it through the pita to eat.

→ INGREDIENTS

- 4 eggplants (aubergine), roasted and peeled
- Spray olive oil
- 4 garlic cloves, crushed
- 1 teaspoon salt
- 120 ml (4 fl oz) tahini
- 1 teaspoon ground cumin
- 50 ml (1.7 fl oz) lemon juice, fresh
- Olive oil
- Sourdough bread slices, 2 cm (1 in) thick or traditional pita bread

→ METHOD

Cut the eggplants in half lengthwise and score the flesh into diamonds. Spray the cut side of the eggplants with oil and cook on the grill for 25–30 minutes, turning regularly.

Lift the eggplants from the barbecue and allow to cool for 10 minutes before peeling the skin away from the flesh. Alternatively, scoop/scrape the flesh from the charred skin with a spoon.

Blend the cooked eggplant, garlic, salt, tahini, cumin and lemon juice to a smooth paste.

Grill the sliced bread or pita bread, sprayed with oil, until marked and serve warm with room temperature Baba Ganoush.

TINY ARANCINI
MAKES 16

Leftover risotto will store in the refrigerator for up to four days. A cooked risotto can be turned out into a springform tin and allowed to set overnight. It can then be cut into wedges and char-grilled or pan-fried. The arancini will not look cooked on the side but that is okay because the flavour and texture will be set by the flat sides of each one. I have made these with a cube of mozarella in the middle, replacing the salami.

→ INGREDIENTS

- 400 g (14 oz) basic risotto (see below)
- 16 x 1 cm (½ in) cubed pieces of salami
- Breadcrumbs

FOR THE RISOTTO

- 60g (2oz) butter
- 1 small onion, chopped
- 1 clove garlic, chopped
- 320 g (11 oz) arborio rice
- 1 L (33 fl oz) boiling chicken stock
- 2 teaspoons salt
- ½ teaspoon white pepper
- 3 tablespoons parmesan cheese, grated
- 2 tablespoons parsley, finely chopped

→ METHOD

Melt 30g (1oz) of the butter in a large heavy saucepan and cook onion and garlic. When onion is soft and golden, add the rice and fry for 2 minutes, stirring constantly, then pour in 1 ladle of boiling stock and cook gently, while stirring, until it is absorbed.

Continue cooking gently, adding stock a cupful at a time and stirring constantly for 15–20 minutes or until rice is tender and all liquid is absorbed. Season with salt and pepper, stir in remaining butter and the cheese. Cover with a lid and leave risotto to sit for 3 minutes before serving.

This will make 900g (2lb) of risotto.

To make the arancini, divide the 400g (14oz) of required risotto into 16 equal portions. Put one cube of salami into the middle of the mixture and roll/shake the rice into a ball. Flatten into a round of 4cm (1.7in) in diameter and 2cm (1in) thick, then roll in breadcrumbs. Make sure all excess breadcrumbs are removed.

To barbecue, spray a medium-hot plate with oil and place on the arancini. Cook for 1 minute. Spray liberally with oil and turn and cook for another minute on the other flat side. Lift the browned arancini onto a plate and leave for 2 minutes before service.

LAMB KOFTAS WITH PITA BREAD, YOGHURT & MINT

SERVES 4

When cooking items like this on the grill, be aware that the bamboo skewers catch light very easily. The alternative is to use metal skewers, which is also better environmentally.

→ INGREDIENTS

- 20 g (0.7 oz) burghul (cracked wheat)
- 1 tablespoon olive oil, plus extra to brush
- 1 small onion, finely chopped
- 2 garlic cloves, crushed
- 1 x 3 cm (1 in) piece ginger, peeled, finely grated
- 2 teaspoons ground coriander
- ½ teaspoon ground cinnamon
- 500 g (18 oz) ground lamb, no fat
- 1 egg yolk
- 2 tablespoons pine nuts, chopped
- 2 tablespoons freshly chopped coriander, plus extra coriander leaves to serve
- Sea salt
- Freshly ground black pepper
- 8–12 wooden skewers, soaked in cold water for 30 minutes
- Spray oil
- Pita bread, yoghurt and mint leaves, to serve

→ METHOD

Soak the burghul in cold water for 30 minutes, drain and squeeze dry.

Cook onion in heated oil for 3 minutes or until onion is soft. Add the garlic, ginger and spices and stir for a further minute. Allow to cool.

Place the burghul, onion mixture, lamb, egg yolk, pine nuts and coriander in a large bowl. Using hands, mix until all ingredients are well combined. Season with salt and pepper.

Wet your hands and shape the mixture around the skewer tip (the pointy end) in a small sausage shape. Refrigerate for at least 2 hours before use.

To cook, brush with a little olive oil and put onto a medium-hot plate. Cook the koftas for 5 minutes, turning occasionally until golden brown. Move to hot grill to crisp and brown even more.

Serve with pita bread, yoghurt, mint and coriander.

CHEESY CREAMY POTATOES
SERVES 6

→ INGREDIENTS

- 1 kg (35 oz) potatoes, washed (use Pontiac or regular ones)
- 1 tablespoon butter
- 125 g (4.5 oz) onion, finely chopped
- 100 ml (3.5 fl oz) cream whisked with

- 350 ml (12 fl oz) milk
- Sea salt to taste
- Ground white pepper to taste
- 125 g (4.5 oz) Gruyere cheese, grated

→ METHOD

Slice the potatoes very finely (use a knife or mandolin) – put into water to stop browning.

Grease a suitably sized ovenproof dish with the butter and sprinkle in a layer of onion then layer in half the potatoes. Pour in half the cream/milk mixture. Wriggle/shake the dish so the liquid goes all the way through and sprinkle with a little salt and pepper. Add the last of the onion and the potatoes and the cream and milk.

Sprinkle with a little more salt and pepper, top with the cheese and cook at 180°C for 1 hour or until soft when a sharp knife is inserted. Remove from oven to serve.

SKEWERED PRAWNS, BARBECUED LEMON
SERVES 4

→ INGREDIENTS

- 16 medium green king prawns, peeled and de-veined
- Bamboo skewers, soaked in water for 30 minutes or metal ones
- 4 lemon cheeks
- Olive oil
- Salt and pepper to taste

→ METHOD

Insert the skewer into tail of the prawn and thread the meat on so that the flesh is kept straight. Arrange on a flat plate and drizzle over light olive oil. Rotate the prawns to coat them with oil.

Put the lemon cheeks onto the medium-hot grill, cut-side down, and cook for 1 minute.

Place the prawns on a medium-hot plate and cook for 3 minutes. Turn the prawns constantly and drizzle with the oil they have been sitting in. Sprinkle with salt and pepper.

To serve, remove the skewers from the prawns and put onto individual plates with a little side salad. Decorate with lemon cheek showing the barbecue marking. Alternatively, you can leave the skewers in and put on a platter, decorated with the lemon cheeks, and serve around the barbie as guests are assembling.

OYSTERS WITH GARLIC OIL & PRESERVED LEMON
SERVES 4

Preserved lemon can be very strong in flavour so use sparingly.

→ INGREDIENTS

- 24 large oysters, freshly shucked
- Garlic oil
- Rock salt
- Preserved lemon rind to taste, washed and minced or very finely sliced
- Cracked black pepper

→ METHOD

Place the oysters onto a hot grill and drizzle with a little garlic oil. Cook for 1–2 minutes. The rim of the oyster flesh should start to bubble, which indicates the oysters are ready to serve.

Serve the oysters on a bed of rock salt (to stop them slipping) on individual plates. Top with preserved lemon and sprinkle with cracked pepper. Be mindful that the shells are very hot to handle and will continue cooking for a couple of minutes after they have been removed from the heat.

THE BEST GARLIC BREAD
SERVES 8

→ INGREDIENTS

- 250 g (9 oz) salted butter, room temperature
- 6 cloves garlic
- 3 tablespoons parsley, chopped
- 1 tablespoon lemon zest, finely grated
- 1 tablespoon lemon juice
- ½ tablespoon black pepper, freshly ground
- 1 loaf day-old bread of any type

→ METHOD

Put all ingredients, except for the bread, into a large bowl or a processor. Combine well – if using a bowl, best to mash with a large fork and for the processor, just pulse until smooth. Lift out with a spatula and store or use.

The secret to the best garlic bread is to smear both sides of the bread and cook on a hot flat plate until lightly browned – finish by crisping on the open grill.

MEATBALLS & BARBECUE SAUCE
MAKES 20–24

To make it easy to roll the meatballs, dip your hands into a bowl of cold water and then start the rolling process.

→ INGREDIENTS

- 500 g (16 oz) lean minced beef
- 3 tablespoons green spring onions, chopped
- 1 teaspoon pre-prepared curry powder
- 40 g (1.5 oz) cous cous, hydrated
- 1 teaspoon oregano, chopped
- 1 egg
- 120 ml (4 fl oz) barbecue sauce

→ METHOD

Combine all the ingredients, excluding the sauce, and mix well using your hands.

Roll into 3cm (1in) diameter meatballs (around 25g/1oz each). Cover and refrigerate for 2 hours.

Spray a hot plate with oil. Add the meatballs and turn regularly to cook for 5–7 minutes.

Place meatballs on a platter and serve with the sauce to one side.

TINY SAUSAGES & CAPSICUM PEPPER SAUCE
SERVES 4

This sauce is great as a base for pizza instead of the usual tomato sauce and is sensational with barbecued lamb chops.

→ INGREDIENTS

- 16 tiny sausages/chippolatas
- 150 ml (5 fl oz) roasted capsicum pepper sauce (see below)
- Spray oil

CAPSICUM PEPPER SAUCE

- 5 medium red capsicums (peppers), deseeded and roughly chopped
- 2 medium onions, roughly chopped

- 4 large cloves garlic, crushed
- 2 tablespoons thyme
- 250 ml (8 fl oz) white wine
- 250 ml (8 fl oz) cider vinegar
- ½ teaspoon salt
- ½ teaspoon cayenne pepper
- 250 ml (8 fl oz) olive oil

→ METHOD

Spray the hot plate of a barbecue with oil and cook the sausages for 3–4 minutes or until done. Lift onto some paper towels. Serve the sausages with a bowl of the sauce at one end of the platter.

FOR THE CAPSICUM PEPPER SAUCE

Put the red capsicums, onions, garlic, thyme, wine and vinegar into a large pot. Simmer for 45 minutes. Remove the lid for the last 10 minutes of cooking to allow evaporation. You should have about ½ cup cooking liquid left when you finish the cooking. Add the salt and cayenne pepper.

Blend the capsicum mixture in processor or blender. When finely pureed, slowly pour in the oil as you blend. Strain (optional) and test for seasoning.

Pour into a sterilised jar and refrigerate when cool. It will store for up to 7 days.

SEA SCALLOPS, PARLSEY & MACADAMIA PESTO
SERVES 4

→ INGREDIENTS

- 16 sea scallops
- Spray olive oil
- Sea salt
- 100 g (3.5 oz) iceberg lettuce, finely shredded, middle leaves only
- 160 g (5.5 oz) ripe Roma tomatoes, flesh only and finely diced
- 1 tablespoon dill, finely chopped
- 4 tablespoons parsley & macadamia pesto
- Ground black pepper

PARSLEY & MACADAMIA PESTO

- 40 g (1.5 oz) parsley sprigs, washed and tightly packed into the cup
- 1 tablespoon macadamia nuts, roughly chopped, roasted, unsalted
- 180 ml (6 fl oz) macadamia nut oil
- 1 large clove garlic, crushed
- 30g (1oz) parmesan cheese, finely grated

→ METHOD

Trim the scallops of the black membrane on the side. Spray each one and cook on hot flat plate for 1–1½ minutes each side depending on the thickness of each scallop. Turn and cook for no more than 1 minute on the other side.

Scallops must not be overcooked and prefer to be seared rather than cooked through as they go very tough when overcooked. Sprinkle with salt only as you cook.

To serve, put equal amount of the finely shredded lettuce in small piles around the perimeter of individual dinner plates. Top with scallops, sprinkle on the tomato dices that have been mixed with the dill.

Spoon an equal amount of pesto onto the centre of each plate. Grind black pepper over the plate and serve immediately.

FOR THE PARSLEY AND MACADAMIA PESTO

Put all ingredients into a processor bowl. Pulse the processor until the ingredients start to break down then leave the engine to run to form a smooth paste. Adjust the consistency of the pesto with more oil if needed.

ATLANTIC SALMON RISOTTO CAKES
MAKES 24

The basic mixture with the salmon added is quite sticky so it is best to divide the mixture into the 24 portions using a small ice-cream scoop or a spoon dipped in water. Dip your hands in water too before you roll and flaten the balls. I sometimes don't use the breadcrumbs and the cakes still cook nicely.

→ INGREDIENTS

- 500 g (18 oz) basic risotto, cooled (see below)
- 1 tablespoon lemon zest, finely grated
- 100 g (4 oz) Atlantic salmon, boneless, skinless and finely chopped
- 2 eggs
- 45 g (1.5 oz) plain flour
- 1 teaspoon powdered dill
- Breadcrumbs
- Spray olive oil

BASIC RISOTTO

- 30 g (1 oz) butter
- 3 tablespoons onions, finely chopped
- 2 cloves garlic, chopped
- 215 g (7.5 oz) Italian arborio rice
- 1 L (34 fl oz) boiling fish/prawn stock
- 3 tablespoons parmesan cheese, finely grated
- 1 teaspoon salt
- ½ teaspoon white pepper

→ METHOD

Melt butter in a large heavy saucepan and fry onion and garlic until soft and golden. Stir in the rice and fry for 3 minutes, stirring constantly, then add 1 ladel of boiling stock and cook, while stirring, until it is absorbed. Add stock a ladel at a time and stir constantly for 15–20 minutes or until rice is tender and all liquid is absorbed and the risotto is creamy and white.

Stir in cheese, salt, pepper and dill. Cover with lid and leave risotto to sit for 3 minutes.

Mix the risotto with the zest, salmon, eggs, flour and dill and stir well. Divide the risotto into 24 equal portions and roll into balls. Flatten into patties of 4cm (2in) in diameter, then coat in breadcrumbs. Spray a flat plate liberally with oil, add the cakes and cook for 1 minute. Spray liberally with oil, turn and cook for another minute on the other flat side. Serve as a pass-round or in the middle of the table with a tossed salad.

CHICKEN KOFTAS
SERVES 4

→ INGREDIENTS

- 500 g (17 oz) chicken, finely minced
- 1 onion, finely chopped
- 1 chilli, seeded and chopped
- 2 tablespoons fresh mint, chopped
- ½ teaspoon salt
- 1 teaspoon garam masala
- ½ teaspoon coriander powder
- ½ teaspoon cumin powder
- 30 g (1 oz) dried breadcrumbs
- Bamboo skewers
- Spray oil
- Mint sprigs for decoration

→ METHOD

Mix chicken with onion, chilli, mint, salt, garam masala, coriander, cumin and breadcrumbs. Knead mixture until stiff and smooth.

Shape the chicken mixture into a small sausage size around one end of the bamboo skewer. The meat mixture should be around 3cm (1in) in diameter and 8cm (3in) long.

Lay the koftas on a cling wrap-covered plate. Cover and refrigerate for 1 hour.

Spray the koftas with oil and cook on a medium-hot plate. Turn every minute until cooked, 8–10 minutes.

Serve on platter decorated with mint sprigs.

SCALLOPS & ANCHOVY SAUCE
SERVES 4

→ INGREDIENTS

- 16 scallops, roe on
- 60 ml (2 fl oz) good mayonnaise
- 1 tablespoon lemon juice
- 1 tablespoon cold water
- 4 anchovy fillets, mashed
- 16 small sprigs dill

→ METHOD

Trim the scallops by removing the black membrane from the side of the scallop.

Make the anchovy sauce by blending the mayonnaise, lemon juice, water, anchovies and dill to a smooth consistency.

Spray the scallops with oil and cook on a very hot plate for 1–1½ minutes. Turn and cook for no more than 1 minute on this side.

Spoon a small amount of the sauce into the base of Chinese spoons or dessert spoons.

Place a scallop on top and spoon over a little of the sauce. Decorate with the dill sprig.

Serve on a platter with the handles facing to the rim.

CURRIED ZUCCHINI PAPPADUM STACK
SERVES 4

→ INGREDIENTS

- 4 medium yellow or green zucchinis (courgettes) or both
- 3 tablespoons vegetable oil
- 1 teaspoon black mustard seed
- 1 tablespoon Indian curry powder
- 1 red capsicum (pepper), cheeks only

- 1 small onion, peeled
- Salt to taste
- 12 small pappadums
- Spray oil
- 200 g (7 oz) natural yoghurt
- Indian mango pickle

→ METHOD

Trim the zucchinis and cut down the centre lengthwise. Cut these halves into half moons around 2cm (1in) long. Pour the oil into a bowl and mix in the mustard seeds and curry powder. Dice the flesh of the capsicum and onion and add to the oil mixture. Now add the zucchini and toss to coat. Leave to sit for 1 hour before cooking

Spray both sides of the pappadums liberally with oil and put onto a hot grill. Do only a couple at a time so you can turn them quickly. They crisp and sizzle very quickly so be ready to turn. Drain on kitchen towel.

Tip the zucchini mixture onto the flat plate of a barbecue. Allow to cook through, turning regularly; sprinkle with salt to taste. The zucchini is cooked more quickly by dropping the barbecue hood. When soft, remove from barbecue with as much of the cooking juices as possible.

Put some natural yoghurt into the centre of the individual plates and place a pappadum. Spoon over some zucchini mixture and add another pappadum. Spoon over a little more of the zucchini and top with a pappadum. Repeat until the four plates are done.

Serve with the Indian mango pickle and yoghurt on the side.

BALSAMIC ASPARAGUS
SERVES 4

→ **INGREDIENTS**

- 12 green asparagus spears
- 1 egg yolk
- 30 ml (1 fl oz) verjuice
- 10 ml (0.3 fl oz) balsamic vinegar

→ **METHOD**

Trim asparagus and cook in boiling water for 2–3 minutes depending on size and thickness.

In the meantime, whisk the egg yolk, verjuice and balsamic vinegar over the boiling water until thickened and light in colour.

Keep sauce warm and lift asparagus from water and run under cold water to stop cooking. Serve the asparagus in the centre of the table and with warm balsamic sauce on the side.

ASPARAGUS, PRAWNS, BOCCONCINI, MIXED LEAVES AND SALSA VERDE

`SERVES 4`

→ INGREDIENTS

- 1 bag (100g (3.5 oz)) mixed lettuce leaves
- 16 medium asparagus spears, trimmed and cooked
- 16 medium king prawns, cooked, peeled and vein removed
- 20 g (0.7 oz) bocconcini, sliced
- 1 medium-sized bunch Italian parsley, leaves only
- 30 g (1 oz) pickled gherkins, roughly chopped
- 30 g (1 oz) capers, rinsed
- 1 clove garlic, chopped
- 1 tablespoon olive oil
- 2 tablespoons lemon juice
- 120 ml (4 fl oz) water

→ METHOD

Layer, in equal amounts, the leaves, asparagus, prawns and bocconcini onto individual plates.

Make the salsa by putting the parsley, gherkins, capers and garlic into a food processor. Process for 30 seconds, add the oil, juice, 120 ml (4 fl oz) of water and ground black pepper to taste. Process again until smooth and runny. Drizzle over the salad ingredients or serve separately.

MUSHROOM AND COTTAGE CHEESE PATÉ WITH MOUNTAIN BREAD CHIPS

MAKES 600 G (20 OZ)

This paté is great for a large group of people and it also makes very good individual serves if you want to use it as an entree. I have done them individually and, when cooled, have topped them with parsley and melted gelatine. Looks good!

→ INGREDIENTS

- 1 teaspoon olive oil
- 100 g (3.5 oz) onions, roughly chopped
- 300 g (10 oz) large mushrooms, roughly chopped
- 60 ml (2 fl oz) fat-free milk
- 1 teaspoon cumin powder
- ½ teaspoon mixed spice
- 250 g (9 oz) low-fat cottage cheese
- 5 g (0.1 oz) gelatine powder
- 2 sheets fat-free flat bread wraps (lavash or mountain bread)

→ METHOD

Preheat oven to 160°C. Heat the oil in a small pan, add the onions and mushrooms and cook for 2 minutes, stirring all the time. Pour in the milk and simmer until the mushrooms start to collapse. Remove from the heat to cool for 3 minutes.

Tip the cooled mushroom mix into a processor bowl and add the cumin, mixed spice and the cheese. Add ground black pepper to taste.

Melt the gelatine in warm water and whisk to dissolve, pour into the processor and work into a paste. Don't overprocess as it is good to have flecks of the white in the dark mixture.

Spoon the mushroom pate into individual bowls or storage bowls. I used small glass bowls that take a cup and a bit each. Cover and refrigerate.

Cut the wraps into strips about 4 cm (1.5 in) wide, then into triangles. Place on baking-paper-lined baking tray and crisp in the oven – around 15–20 minutes. They keep beautifully in an airtight container if you don't use them all. Serve these in a bowl in the middle of the table with the paté.

BARBECUED HERB PRAWN KEBABS

SERVES 4

These make an ideal snack if you have some time on your hands... and your visitors will love them!

→ INGREDIENTS

- 8 medium-large green king prawns, peeled and de-veined
- 2 tablespoons parsley, chopped
- 1 tablespoon dill, chopped
- 2 tablespoons chervil, chopped
- 1 teaspoon allspice
- 70 ml (2.5 fl oz) grapefruit juice
- 8 skewers, metal or bamboo
- Spray light olive oil

→ METHOD

Preheat barbeque to medium.

Ensure the prawns are clean – place in a glass/stainless steel bowl.

Add the parsley, dill, chervil, allspice and juice to them and tumble to coat. Leave to sit for 30 minutes.

Thread each prawn onto a skewer (see note below), spray with oil and cook on a hot plate on the barbeque for 2–3 minutes or until done. Serve immediately.

The prawns are threaded on by inserting the sharp point of the skewer into the tail end of the prawn then pushing it up through the prawn to keep it as straight as possible; you remove the curl of each prawn by doing this. If you are using wooden or bamboo skewers, soak them in water for around 30 minutes before use.

MEXICAN CHILLI SWEET POTATO WEDGIES

→ INGREDIENTS

- 400 g (14 oz) sweet potato, peeled and cut into wedges
- Spray light olive oil
- 1–2 teaspoons Mexican spice mix powder

→ METHOD

Preheat oven to 200°C and line a large baking tray with baking paper.

Spray the wedges, in a bowl, with minimal oil and sprinkle over spice mix powder – toss to coat then tip onto baking tray. Make sure there is a single layer and pieces are not on top of each other.

Cook for 30 minutes and turn only once during that time – and serve when ready.

The cooking time will vary according to the size of the wedges – the larger and more chunky, the longer cooking will be needed. You can serve these with low-fat sour cream.

OYSTERS IN PROSCIUTTO

SERVES 4

→ INGREDIENTS

- 24 freshly shucked oysters, out of shell
- 24 x 10 cm long slices prosciutto
- toothpicks
- Olive oil spray
- 2 lemon cheeks

→ METHOD

Wrap each oyster loosely in a piece of prosciutto and secure with a toothpick.

Spray the flat plate with a little oil and cook on medium temperature flat plate until crisp, around 2–3 minutes.

Put onto platter, squeeze with lemon and pass round as you barbecue.

KING PRAWNS, MINT AND CHERVIL SAUCE
SERVES 4

→ INGREDIENTS

- 16 medium king prawns, completely peeled and deveined
- 2 tablespoons oil
- ½ teaspoon each of salt
- ½ lemon cracked pepper

MINT AND CHERVIL SAUCE

- 1 tablespoon eschalot, finely chopped
- 2 tablespoons fresh mint, chopped
- 1 tablespoon fresh chervil, chopped
- 1 small sprig fresh thyme
- 2 tablespoons white vinegar
- 2 tablespoons white wine
- 2 egg yolks
- 125 g (4 oz) butter, cut into cubes
- ½ teaspoon lemon juice
- Salt and cayenne pepper to taste
- 1 tablespoon each of fresh mint and chervil, broken or chopped

→ METHOD

Make the sauce by putting the eschalots, mint, chervil, thyme, vinegar and white wine into a saucepan, bring to the boil and reduce by two thirds. Remove from the heat and transfer to the top of a double boiler. Cool, add the egg yolks and whisk.

Place over simmering water and whisk until the mixture thickens, then start to whisk in the butter until all is used. Remove from heat and add the lemon juice and salt and pepper to taste. Strain and stir in the broken mint and chervil.

Toss the prawns in oil, salt and lemon pepper. Sit for 15 minutes. Cook the prawns on a hot plate and turn regularly to cook through – they will take only a couple of minutes. Remove from the heat.

Serve the prawns on individual plates and with the sauce spooned over. Sprinkle with a little more cracked pepper to decorate.

MEAT

BARBECUE LAMB SANDWICH WITH MAYO
SERVES 4

→ INGREDIENTS

- 4 x 150 g (5 oz) lamb steaks
- 1 tablespoon cracked lemon pepper
- 4 large cos lettuce leaves, crisp and roughly sliced
- 16 pieces semi-roasted tomatoes
- 4 bocconcini, sliced into flat rounds
- Flat bread such as ciabatta, sourdough or focaccia, cut into 4 equal pieces to suit size of steaks
- Spray oil
- Mayonnaise

→ METHOD

Sprinkle the lamb steaks on both sides with the cracked lemon pepper.

Spray the lamb steaks with oil and cook on the barbecue for 2 minutes on one side, turn, cook one further minute, then lift to plate and let rest for 1 minute before assembling the sandwich.

Slice the flat bread pieces into halves and spray with oil to grill cut-side down. When charred, turn and mark/brown the other side of the bread.

To assemble the sandwich, take the base piece of bread and spread on some mayonnaise and put on an individual plate. Equally distribute the cos and semi-roasted tomatoes on top of the base. Place the steaks on top and then a few slices of the bocconcini cheese.

BARBECUED SIRLOIN & GREEN CURRY DRESSING

→ ## INGREDIENTS

- 750 g (26 oz) sirloin steak, in one piece with all fat and connective tissue removed
- Spray oil
- 120 ml (4 fl oz) coconut cream
- 240 ml (8 fl oz) green curry paste
- 80 g (3 oz) roasted peanuts, no skins and roughly chopped
- 480 ml (16 fl oz) coconut milk

- 1 tablespoon raw sugar or palm sugar
- 1 teaspoon salt or fish sauce
- 3 long green chillies, seeded and cut into fine strips
- 3 kaffir lime leaves, vein removed and cut into fine strips
- Fresh coriander leaves

→ ## METHOD

Make sure the beef is completely trimmed – refrigerate until ready to cook.

Make the dressing by bringing the coconut cream to the boil in a wok and cook for a minute–the cream will separate – then add the green curry paste and stir for 2 minutes. The liquid will become very fragrant.

Add two-thirds of the peanuts and the coconut milk and cook until heated through. Tip in the sugar and salt/fish sauce and stir. The liquid should now be heated, salty and sweet so adjust the flavours to your liking. Add the chillies and kaffir lime leaves, then remove from heat and stir for a minute.

Remove the beef from the refrigerator 10 minutes before use. Spray the beef with oil, put onto the very hot plate on a barbecue and seal for a minute on all sides. Then lift onto medium-hot grill and cook for 5–10 minutes on each side or until medium rare. This will depend on the thickness of the beef. Remove and let sit in a warm place for 20 minutes.

When the beef is ready, thinly slice and pack onto a shallow plate. Pour over the curry sauce, sprinkle in the remaining peanuts and rip the coriander leaves over the beef and sauce. Serve with steamed fragrant rice.

CHILLI LAMB SKEWERS & ASIAN SLAW
SERVES 4

The addition of lemon to the lamb is an old favourite of lamb eaters – the Greeks love it with barbecued lamb. The acid (from the squeezed lemon juice) cuts down the fat in this recipe so the fat is almost non-existent. I like to make the slaw and use immediately. It loses its crunch if you let it sit for any period of time with the dressing. If you are serving this to guests, you can have the cabbage partly done, covered with cling wrap and refrigerated, and the same for the dressing. Mix to combine as you need this delicious slaw.

→ INGREDIENTS

- 500 g (18 oz) lean lamb strips
- 4 stainless steel skewers (lightly oiled) or bamboo skewers that have been soaked in water for 30 minutes
- ½ teaspoon chilli powder
- 4 lime cheeks

ASIAN SLAW
- 1 kg (35 oz) shredded Chinese cabbage
- 25 g (0.9 oz) finely sliced spring onions

- 1 red capsicum (pepper), diced
- 60g (2oz) snow pea sprouts
- 60 ml (2 fl oz) low-salt soy sauce
- 1 tablespoon green ginger, minced
- 1 small red chilli, seeds in and minced
- 1 teaspoon sesame oil
- 1 teaspoon palm sugar
- 2 tablespoon lime juice

→ METHOD

Buy the lamb already in strips if you like; however it is best to cut them from lamb mini roasts which I use to get 2 cm (1 in) strips. Thread equal amounts on to skewers in an 'S' shape. Sprinkle evenly with the chilli and let sit for 5 minutes.

Make the slaw by combining the cabbage, onion, capsicum and snow pea sprouts. In a separate container, mix the soy, ginger, chilli, oil, sugar and lime juice. Stir well and pour over the cabbage mix and toss well.

Cook the oil-sprayed lamb on a medium-hot plate which will cook in 5 minutes or leave longer for well done. Serve each skewer of lamb on top of equal amounts of slaw and with a lime cheek on each plate.

CHAR-ROASTED GOAT RACK WITH GARLIC THYME BASTE, BARBECUED ONIONS & BROCCOLINI

SERVES 4

→ INGREDIENTS

BARBECUED ONIONS

- 600 g (21 oz) onions, peeled and sliced into rings
- 1 tablespoon oil
- 1 tablespoon butter
- 375 ml (13 fl oz) beer
- Salt, optional

- 2 x 8 cutlet racks of goat
- 3 large garlic cloves, finely minced
- 1 tablespoon lemon thyme or thyme, fresh and minced
- 1 teaspoon ground black pepper
- 80 ml (2.8 fl oz) vegetable oil
- 2 bunches broccolini, trimmed

→ METHOD

Seal the racks on a hot grill, starting with skin side down, for 2 minutes; turn and cook for another 2 minutes. Lift them onto a baking tray and let cool for 5 minutes.

Mix the garlic, thyme, pepper and oil. Baste the goat thickly with it and roast at 150–160°C with the hood down on the barbecue. I do mine by sitting the tray on a cooling rack on the plate with the two grill burners on medium. Cook for 5 minutes and then baste again to continue cooking for another 8–12 minutes. It should take about 12 minutes to reach 65°C internal temperature but that time will vary depending on thickness of the racks.

Remove when cooked to your liking and rest for at least 5 minutes to set the juices.

Boil the broccolini until done, then drain and serve in the centre of individual plates. Top with barbecued onion and cut the cutlets to sit around and on the onions.

FOR THE BARBECUED ONIONS

Sprinkle the onions with a little salt if you desire. Melt the oil and butter on a medium-hot plate and add the onions. Move around the plate with the spatula and let them lightly brown. Pour a third of the beer over the onions. Stir the onions around and drop the barbecue hood or cover with a large stainless steel bowl. Leave the onions to stew in their own juices and add the beer as they start to dry, still turning regularly. When done, remove from barbecue and keep warm until ready to serve.

OLIVE PARSLEY LAMB WITH WHITE TURNIP STEW

SERVES 4

→ INGREDIENTS

- 2 x 200 g (7 oz) mini lamb roasts
- 1½ tablespoons smooth French mustard
- 4 tablespoons olive parsley paste (see below)
- 120 g (4 oz) onion, roughly chopped
- 150 g (5.3 oz) celery, roughly diced
- 400 g (14 oz) white turnip, roughly diced
- vegetable stock, made from 1 vegetable stock cube, around 500 ml (17 fl oz)
- ½ teaspoon ground white pepper

OLIVE PARSLEY PASTE

- 80 g (2.8 oz) green olives
- 50 g (1.8 oz) curly parsley
- 1 tablespoon fresh oregano
- 2 lemons, grated zest only
- Juice of 1 lemon
- 3 cloves garlic, chopped
- 1 tablespoon hazlenuts, skins on and roughly chopped

→ METHOD

To make the olive parsley paste put all ingredients into a processor and work to a rough paste.

Pre heat oven to 180ºC. Trim all fat from the lamb. Mix the mustard with olive parsley paste and smear over the top lamb. Leave to sit for 5 minutes.

Put a cooling rack onto a baking tray and place the lamb onto the rack. Cook for 40 minutes or until done to your liking. Remove from oven to rest for 10 minutes before slicing.

Meanwhile cook the onion, celery and turnips in the vegetable stock. Just cover the mixed vegetables and simmer until done: 15–20 minutes. Add the white pepper towards the end of the cooking.

Serve vegetables onto dinner plates. Slice the lamb roasts around 2cm (0.8 in) thick and serve equal amounts of it on top of the vegetables.

Watch the white pepper as it builds in intensity as it cooks and lingers on the palate.

I just love the white turnip stew and I use the leftovers on rye toast (or similar) for breakfast the next morning (if there is any left that is).

BARBECUE BEEF STIR FRY
SERVES 4

→ INGREDIENTS

- 500 g (1lb) beef strips, either rump or sirloin
- 1 teaspoon ground allspice
- 60 ml (2 fl oz) soy sauce
- 1 tablespoon mirin
- 1 tablespoon peanut oil
- 1 medium-sized red chilli, seeded and finely chopped
- 2 coriander roots, washed and finely chopped
- 1 tablespoon palm sugar
- 1 small onion, cut into wedges
- 50 g (1.8 oz) bean sprouts
- 8 water chestnuts, finely sliced
- 50 g (1.8 oz) coriander

→ METHOD

Put the meat in a bowl and sprinkle with allspice.

Combine the soy, mirin, oil, chilli, coriander root and palm sugar. Mix well to dissolve the sugar. Pour over the meat, cover and leave to sit for one hour. Drain the meat, reserving the soy mixture.

Spray the flat barbecue plate liberally with oil. Add meat strips immediately. Put onions on another part of the sprayed plate and turn both meat and onions regularly for two minutes. Do not combine.

Add bean sprouts and water chestnuts to onions; lift and toss to combine all ingredients, including the meat, in a concentrated area on the barbecue.

Spoon over some of the reserved marinade and lift and toss for another two minutes. Lift into a serving bowl, add the coriander leaves and toss gently.

Serve stir-fry with boiled rice or rice noodles

THE PERFECT BARBECUE STEAK
SERVES 4

No barbecue would be complete without a definitive steak. Over the many years that I have cooked beef steak on the barbecue, I know this is the best method. Of course, choosing the correct beef cut is really crucial to the finished product. Cook your steak this way and never serve it any further cooked than medium.

You will have noticed that I have advised leaving some fat on the steak. This is essential for flavour complexity. If you prefer your meat without the fat, you may slice it off after the cooking has happened.

Marbled beef is identified by streaks of white through the red meat. These are thin lines of fat which melt in the cooking process and give that superb flavour of barbecue beef steak.

→ INGREDIENTS

- 4 x 4 cm (2 in) thick sirloin steaks, well marbled
- Salt and ground black pepper
- Light olive oil

→ METHOD

Trim as much fat from your steaks as you like but ensure that at least ½ cm (¼ in) is left. Importantly, always remove the meat you will barbecue from the refrigerator at least 10 minutes before use.

Spray the steaks with oil and place onto the very hot plate. Leave to sit for 2 minutes without disturbing the meat. Do not at any time puncture the steaks with forks or knives or you will release the vital juices of the meat.

Spray the steaks lightly with oil and turn onto another part of the very hot plate. If there is not enough room, lift each piece of meat and let the plate recover its heat so it can seal the meat on this side just as it did for the first side. Cook a further 2 minutes.

Flip the steaks again but this time onto the grill and cook for 2 minutes each side, sprinkling with salt and pepper as you turn them.

Remove and allow to rest for at least 5 minutes before serving. This gives the meat a chance to set and means that the red juices do not run all over the plate.

Serve the steak onto individual plates with vegetables or salad of your choice and at least one good mustard.

CHILLI BEEF STRIP TACOS
SERVES 4

→ INGREDIENTS

- 500 g (17 oz) rump steak
- 2 tablespoons light olive oil
- 2 tablespoons sherry vinegar
- 1 teaspoon Mexican chilli powder
- ½ tablespoon ground allspice
- ½ tablespoon oregano powder
- 1 teaspoon salt
- 100 g (3.5 oz) lettuce, shredded
- 2 medium salad tomatoes, cut into wedges
- 1 large red onion, chopped
- 120 g (4 oz) cheddar cheese, grated
- 2 tablespoons coriander leaves, chopped
- 8 tacos

→ METHOD

Cut the steak across the grain into 1 cm (½ in) wide strips and place in a bowl.

Mix the oil, vinegar, chilli powder, allspice, oregano and salt. Pour over the steak strips and stir to coat the pieces. Cover and refrigerate for at least 2 hours.

Spray the flat plate with oil and tip on the strips. Spread over the plate and cook by tossing and lifting the pieces and allowing them to brown.

The meat will cook in 5–6 minutes and, when done, lift the strips onto a large platter with heaped lettuce, tomatoes, onion and cheese.

Heat 8 taco shells in the barbecue at 180°C.

Serve all the various components in the middle of the table so everyone can stuff their own tacos – meat first into the shell followed by lettuce, tomato, onion, cheese and coriander.

CALVES LIVER WITH SKEWERED ONIONS & CASHEW NUT & MUSTARD BUTTER

SERVES 4

→ INGREDIENTS

- 500 g (17 oz) calves liver, in 1 ½ cm (½ in) thick slices
- 4 small onions, peeled
- Stainless steel skewers
- 8 small potatoes, cut into halves
- Salt
- Smoky paprika powder

CASHEW NUT & MUSTARD BUTTER

- 250 g (9 oz) unsalted butter, room temperature
- 1 tablespoon seeded mustard
- 30 g (1 oz) roasted and salted cashew nuts, finely crushed
- 1 tablespoon fresh parsley, chopped
- 1 tablespoon white vinegar
- ¼ teaspoon freshly ground white pepper

→ METHOD

Put the butter, mustard and crushed nuts into a bowl and start to mash them together. Add the parsley, vinegar and pepper and continue mashing until combined.

Roll into a sausage shape using cling wrap or wax paper and secure by screwing the ends together. Freeze until ready to use.

Make sure the skin is removed from the outside of each slice of liver.

Cut the onions into 1½ cm (½ in) thick rounds and skewer the slices together on the flat.

Boil the potato halves in salted water for 4–5 minutes, drain.

Spray a medium-hot plate with oil and put the skewered onions on. Spray the potatoes and put them on the grill. Sprinkle both with salt and turn frequently to cook.

Once the onions are done, remove and spray the liver with oil and put onto a medium-hot plate. Sprinkle with a little smoky paprika and salt. Turn and do the same to the other side. Liver cooks quickly and it is important to serve it medium because well-done makes the liver too dry and rubbery.

To serve, plate individually by putting four potato pieces into the centre of each plate and top with 1–2 slices of liver. Lay the onion rings beside the liver and potatoes and top the liver with a couple of slices of cashew nut & mustard butter.

BARBECUED LAMB FAJITAS

SERVES 4

→ INGREDIENTS

- 500 g (17 oz) mini lamb roasts
- 1 tablespoon light olive oil
- 2 tablespoons red wine vinegar
- 1 teaspoon Mexican spices
- 1 tablespoon mint, chopped
- 2 tablespoons dried onion flakes
- ¼ teaspoon chilli powder (depends on how 'spicy' your powder is)
- 100 g (3.5 oz) lettuce, shredded
- 120 g (4 oz) carrot, grated
- 2 medium salad tomatoes, cut into wedges
- 120 ml (4 fl oz) reduced fat/light sour cream
- 8 wheat flour tortillas

→ METHOD

Cut the lamb roasts across the grain into 2cm-thick slices, then cut into 1cm-wide strips and place in a bowl. Mix the oil, vinegar, Mexican spices, mint, onion flakes and chilli powder together. Pour over the lamb strips and stir to coat the pieces. Cover and refrigerate for at least 30 minutes to 1 hour.

Tip the strips onto the hot flat plate on the barbecue. Spread over the plate and cook by tossing and lifting the pieces. Allow them to brown, which will take around 5–6 minutes. Spray the tortillas with oil and heat very quickly on the open char grill.

Assemble the fajitas with equal amounts of lettuce, carrot and tomato onto a warmed tortilla. Top with lamb and sour cream. Roll and eat.

I have loved these tasty combinations for years. They are easy and a family favourite. If you can leave the meat to marinade a little longer, they will have a stronger flavour. When you learn how to pronounce them, they are even better. Far-heat-tars may be close.

CARAWAY PORK CUTLETS, BASIL AND TOMATO SLAW
`SERVES 4`

→ INGREDIENTS

- 4–8 pork cutlets, depending on size
- 1 teaspoon caraway seeds
- 250 ml (8 fl oz) beer
- 1 small onion, finely diced
- 2–3 bay leaves
- 1 kg (35 oz) Savoy cabbage, finely shredded
- 50 g (1.8 oz) basil leaves, roughly torn
- 2 large ripe tomatoes, cut into wedges
- 1 small salad onion
- 60 ml (2 fl oz) verjuice
- 2 rashers bacon
- sea salt, to taste

→ METHOD

Trim excess fat from the pork and place in a glass bowl. Add the caraway seeds, beer, small diced onion and the bay leaves. Move the cutlets around and then let them soak in the beer for 10 minutes.

Remove the rind from the bacon rashers and cut into fine strips.

Put the cabbage in a bowl and add the bail leaves and tomatoes. Slice the salad onion into rings and put in with the other 'slaw' ingredients. Pour in the verjuice, olive oil and cooked bacon pieces (see below), add salt and tumble to combine.

Place the strips of bacon on the flat plate, and move them around while they cook until they become crispy. When the bacon is done transfer to a plate lined with paper kitchen towel to cool.

Place the cutlets on the flat plate where the bacon was cooked, and cook on each side for 2 minutes until the meat is sealed. Then spoon a little of the beef and caraway seed mixture onto the pork while it continues to cook.

To finish the cutlets, flash-cook them on both sides on the open slats, then remove from the barbecue.

Serve the pork by spooning some 'slaw' into the centre of each plate and arranging the pork cutlets on top.

BARBECUED BEEF & MUSHROOM KEBABS WITH HOMEMADE BARBECUE SAUCE

SERVES 4

It is recommended by the mushroom growers of Australia to not ever wash mushrooms unless they are to be used immediately. The best way to clean mushrooms if they are to be cleaned at all is to wipe them individually and gently with a damp cloth.

→ INGREDIENTS

HOMEMADE BARBECUE SAUCE

- 240 ml (8 fl oz) orange juice
- 240 ml (8 fl oz) ketchup
- 240 ml (8 fl oz) red wine
- 120 ml (4 fl oz) golden syrup/maple syrup
- 60 ml (2 fl oz) malt vinegar
- 40 g (1.4 oz) onion, chopped

- 600 g (21 oz) rump steak, cut into cubes of 2 cm (1 in)
- 16 button mushrooms, stem removed and wiped clean
- 8 pickled onions, small, cut into halves
- Bamboo or metal skewers – if using bamboo, soak in water for at least 30 minutes
- Salt
- Spray oil

→ METHOD

Thread the different ingredients onto the skewer starting and finishing with a beef cube. Alternate with the mushrooms and the onion halves. Refrigerate until ready to use and then remove for 10 minutes before cooking.

Spray the kebabs with oil and cook on a hot plate for 2 minutes before turning to continue cooking. Sprinkle with salt as you turn.

Lift kebabs from the barbecue and serve with a good potato salad and the sauce on the side.

FOR THE HOMEMADE BARBECUE SAUCE

Make the sauce by blending all ingredients. Pour into a saucepan and simmer to reduce to a consistency of commercial tomato sauce, for about 15–20 minutes.

BONELESS LEG OF LAMB WITH ROSEMARY RUB
SERVES 4

By leaving the meat to sit or rest, the juices settle and the meat carves easily. The juices in the base of the platter are delicious and best spooned over the sliced meat.

→ INGREDIENTS

- 1.5 kg (3 lb) boneless leg of lamb, butterflied
- 15 g (0.5 oz) fresh rosemary leaves only, roughly chopped
- 1 tablespoon celery salt
- ½ teaspoon black pepper, freshly ground
- ½ teaspoon coriander powder
- ½ teaspoon mild Indian curry
- Olive oil
- Pastry brush or similar

→ METHOD

Lay the leg of lamb out as flat as possible and ensure that the meat has an even thickness. This can be difficult as the muscle structure varies and so you may have to slice the meat to flatten it. Skewer into place to maintain a flat appearance.

Mix the rosemary, salt, pepper, coriander and curry. With your fingers, sprinkle/spread half the rub ingredients over the cut side of the lamb and then massage it in.

Put the leg of lamb onto a medium-hot grill cut-side down. Cook for 5 minutes.

Lightly brush the skin side of lamb with oil and turn the leg over to cook for 10–15 minutes with the hood down.

Brush the partially cooked cut side with a little oil and sprinkle over the remaining rub. Turn the meat over again, drop the hood, and leave to cook on the skin side for 10 minutes.

Turn the leg one more time to the open flesh side and cook a further 10–15 minutes with the hood down. Remove from the barbecue and let rest for 5 minutes. Slice the meat and serve with salads or vegetables of your choice.

PROSCIUTTO SAGE LAMB CUTLETS WITH PEA & TOMATO LINGUINE

SERVES 4

→ INGREDIENTS

- 12 large sage leaves
- 12 trimmed medium lamb cutlets
- 12 thin slices parmesan cheese
- 12 slices prosciutto
- Olive oil
- 400 g (14 oz) cooked linguine

- 120 g (4 oz) fresh or frozen peas
- 2 medium ripe tomatoes, diced
- 2 tablespoons pasta tomato sauce
- Lamb or beef stock
- Salt and ground black pepper

→ METHOD

Place a sage leaf on top of each cutlet and an appropriate piece of parmesan cheese (so it covers the leaf and the meat); wrap in a slice of prosciutto.

Cook the lamb cutlets on a medium-hot plate until the cheese is starting to seep through the crisped prosciutto. Remove and keep warm.

Heat enough olive oil in a suitable pan or wok over medium heat. Add the linguine, peas, tomatoes and tomato sauce. Stir and pour in enough stock to make the peas and tomato cook and provide a good sauce for the linguine. Season with salt and pepper to taste.

Serve the linguine in the centre of bowls with the cutlets sitting on top or around the pasta.

ORANGE-SCENTED MEATLOAF & MUSHROOM RAGOUT
SERVES 4–6

If the foil you have on hand is thin, use 2–3 sheets, shiny side in.

→ INGREDIENTS

- 500 g (18 oz) beef, lean minced
- 60 g (2 oz) breadcrumbs, dry
- 1 small onion, chopped
- 1 tablespoon ginger, minced
- 1 tablespoon parsley, chopped
- 1 teaspoon salt
- 1 teaspoon white pepper, ground finely
- 1 tablespoon orange zest, finely grated, and juice of that orange
- 1 large egg, beaten
- 2 tablespoons seeded Dijon mustard
- Olive oil

MUSHROOM RAGOUT

- 1½ tablespoons butter
- 60 g (2oz) spring onions, chopped
- 3 cloves garlic, minced
- 400 g (14 oz) assorted mushrooms, roughly chopped (use wild or exotic mushrooms such as shitake as well as regular ones)
- 300 ml (10 fl oz) demi-glace (from a good deli, butcher or supermarket)
- 60 ml (2 fl oz) red wine
- 1 tablespoon fresh marjoram, chopped
- ½ teaspoon salt

→ METHOD

Combine all the meatloaf ingredients, except for the olive oil, and mix thoroughly. Take a large sheet of thick foil and brush with olive oil. Tip the mixture onto the foil and shape into a sausage shape, 23cm (9in) long by 6cm (2in) in diameter. Wrap the foil around to hold the meat in place and twist the ends to seal. Refrigerate for at least 1 hour.

Prepare the mushroom ragout by melting the butter in a saucepan and add the spring onions and garlic. Cook for 2 minutes. Add the mushrooms, demi-glace and red wine to bring to the boil, then simmer for at least 1 hour. Add the marjoram and salt and cook for a further 5 minutes.

Put the meatloaf onto a medium-hot plate, hood down and cook for 30 minutes, turning every 10 minutes to ensure even cooking. Remove from barbecue and rest for 10 minutes before peeling away the foil. Slice and serve on top of the mushroom ragout.

LAMB CHOPS WITH GREEN BEAN SALAD & SWEET POTATO

SERVES 4

→ INGREDIENTS

- 400 g (14 oz) green beans
- 1 small spanish onion, peeled and finely diced
- 120 ml (4 fl oz) vinaigrette dressing (see recipe below)
- 1 x 350 g (12 oz) sweet potato
- 8 x 100 g (4 oz) lamb loin chops, about 2 cm (1 in) thick
- Spray oil

TRADITIONAL VINAIGRETTE

- 3 tablespoons olive oil
- 1 clove garlic, minced
- ½ teaspoon smooth Dijon mustard
- 2 tablespoons white wine vinegar
- 1 tablespoon parsley, finely chopped
- ½ teaspoon salt
- ¼ teaspoon white pepper

→ METHOD

For the very best results, make the vinaigrette dressing by hand. Put the oil, garlic and mustard in a large bowl and whisk until the mixture is creamy in consistency and light yellow in colour. The whisking aerates and blends extremely well. Whisk in the vinegar and add the parsley and salt and pepper and continue stirring until well mixed.

Top, tail and wash the green beans, place in bowl and pour over boiling water to cover. Leave to sit for 30 seconds, drain and run under very cold water.

Trim the sweet potato if it has thin ends and cook in the microwave at 70% for 4 minutes. Spray with oil, place on a medium grill and cook until done, turning every 5 minutes.

Tip the green beans onto an oiled, medium-hot plate and turn regularly just to heat through – try not to brown. Put the reheated beans into a bowl, add the onion and vinaigrette and toss. Allow to cool.

Grill the chops over medium heat, note there is no need to spray. Cook for 3 minutes on each side or longer if you like.

To serve, slice the sweet potato into even rounds and equally distribute into the centre of individual plates. Top with equal amounts of green bean salad and add two lamb loin chops to each plate.

CHORIZO, MEDITERRANEAN VEGETABLES & GOAT'S CURD PIZZA
SERVES 2–4

→ INGREDIENTS

- 1 pizza base
- Spray oil
- 3 tablespoons tomato cumin pizza base sauce
- 100 g (4 oz) mixed Mediterranean grilled vegetables (from supermarket), roughly chopped
- 100 g (4 oz) Chorizo, finely sliced into rounds
- 100 g (4 oz) goat's curd, from small log
- 1 tablespoon parmesan cheese, finely grated

→ METHOD

Heat pizza stone on grill to high heat for 20 minutes

Put the pizza base on a lightly oil-sprayed pizza tray. Spoon over the tomato cumin sauce.

Evenly spread the vegetables over the tomato topping. Spread the sausage over and around the pizza. Cut the goat's curd into 6 rounds (can be difficult if the cheese is not really firm enough to do this, so you can add dollops if it is easier).

Cook on the pizza stone in the barbecue at 220°C for 7–8 minutes or until the crust is crisp around the edges. Remove from the barbecue and tip onto cutting board. Grate on the parmesan using a microplane or very fine grater; cut into 6–8 wedges and serve on its own as a pass-round or with a salad as a light lunch.

BARBECUED BEEF STEAK, TURMERIC DILL CAULIFLOWER AND GREEN BEANS

SERVES 4

This makes for a more substantial lunch idea!

→ INGREDIENTS

- 4 x 200 g (7 oz) sirloin steaks
- Spray olive oil
- 2 tablespoons olive oil
- 1 teaspoon dill seeds
- 1 teaspoon turmeric powder
- 1 very small cauliflower, stem removed and cut into florets
- 2 tablespoons finely grated lemon zest
- 180 ml (6 fl oz) water
- 250 g (9 oz) green beans, trimmed and cut into 3 cm (1.2 in) pieces
- 1 tablespoon roughly chopped dill

→ METHOD

Trim the steaks if necessary. When ready to cook at the barbecue, spray the steaks with oil and cook on a very hot open grill; when done, remove and rest.

In a wok or large saucepan, pour in the olive oil and heat. Add the dill seeds and turmeric and cook for 1 minute with the lid on. Add the cauliflower and coat it with the dill mixture.

Add the lemon zest and 120 ml (4 fl oz) water; cover and cook at a simmer for 15 minutes, then add the beans with 60 ml (2 fl oz) water and cook until both are tender. Add the dill and stir in. Serve as an accompaniment to the steak.

SPICED YOGHURT PORK FILLET AND PAN-FRIED PEARS

SERVES 4

→ INGREDIENTS

- 600 g (21 oz) pork fillet, cut into medallions
- 150 ml (5 fl oz) no-fat natural yoghurt
- 1 teaspoon smoked paprika powder
- 1 teaspoon fennel seeds, roughly crushed
- 1 teaspoon coriander powder
- ¼ medium onion, finely chopped
- 1 tablespoon minced fresh oregano
- ½ tablespoon mustard seed oil
- lemon flavoured cracked peppercorns
- 8 canned pear halves, well drained
- 120 g (4 oz) cooked silverbeet leaves

→ METHOD

Ensure all fat is removed from the pork medallions. Gently flatten them by pounding with the heel of your hand. Mix the yoghurt, paprika, fennel, coriander, onion and oregano well.

Preheat oven to 180°C. Smear each piece of pork with the yoghurt mixture and leave to sit for 15–30 minutes.

Place the pork into a baking tray and cook in the oven for 15 minutes until firm.

Heat the oil in a non-stick pan, sprinkle the pear halves with cracked pepper and pan-fry to golden brown.

Pile equal amounts of silverbeet onto the centre of each plate, top with equal quantities of pork and two pear halves each. Serve with a fat-free carbohydrate of your choice. I suggest steamed potatoes or basmati rice.

The thickness of each medallion will determine how long they take to cook. Mine were 4–5 cm (1.5–2 in) thick. I had eight of them and they cooked – well spaced on the tray – in the 15 minutes, which left them only just pink and the thinner ones not well done, but just right. It is okay to leave your pork fillet pink.

While testing another batch of this delicious pork dish, I found that the flavour improves if the pork is left in the yoghurt for 45 minutes, but this is dictated by the amount of time you have.

AUSTRALIAN-SPICED BEEF WITH SWEET POTATO MASH
SERVES 4

Australian spices are delicious and give great flavour without salt and the usual seasonings.

→ INGREDIENTS

- 1 x 750 g (26 oz) piece roasting beef (lean topside, fillet or point of rump with fat removed)
- 3 teaspoons ground coriander
- 1 teaspoon ground bush tomato (akudjura)
- ½ teaspoon ground lemon myrtle leaf
- ½ teaspoon wattle seeds, roasted and ground

- ½ teaspoon ground ginger
- ¼ teaspoon ground native pepper berry
- spray olive oil
- 250 g (9 oz) blue pumpkin, peeled and roughly chopped
- 250 g (9 oz) sweet potato, peeled and roughly chopped
- ½ tablespoon extra virgin olive oil
- 250 g (9 oz) broccolini, trimmed

→ METHOD

Preheat oven to 200°C. Trim the beef of all visible fat, mix spices and coat beef. Refrigerate (covered) for 1 hour or longer to dry-marinate. Lift the beef onto a cooking rack and put on a roasting tray, spray with a film of oil and cook for 10 minutes on 200°C, then reduce to 180°C to cook a further 20 minutes or until done to your liking.

Boil the pumpkin and sweet potato until tender; drain and mash with olive oil. Plunge the broccolini into boiling salted water for 1–2 minutes and lift out, drain and serve.

Rest beef for 10 minutes to set the juices, carve into slices and serve resting against an even pile of the mash and broccolini. Pan juices are good with the beef, but as it has loads of flavour, mustards and other condiments are not necessary.

To get the best results from anything you roast, you must have a meat thermometer which gives you internal temperature readings. Note that you will lose around 10 per cent of your meat, in weight, when you roast.

STAR ANISE RACK OF LAMB WITH PEACH RELISH AND PORT JUS

SERVES 4

→ INGREDIENTS

- 4 x three-rib racks of lamb, trimmed, approximately 200 g (7 oz) each rack
- 4 whole star anise
- 2 tablespoons salt-reduced soy sauce
- 120 ml (4 fl oz) mirin
- 60 ml (2 fl oz) port wine
- 400 g (14 oz) sweet potato, roasted
- 300 g (11 oz) green peas, cooked
- 40 g (1.5 oz) peach relish

PEACH RELISH

- 300 g (10.5 oz) dried peaches, chopped
- 30 g (1 oz) raw sugar
- 10 juniper berries
- 240 ml (8 fl oz) white vinegar
- 2 teaspoons grated orange zest
- 1 teaspoon cardamom
- ½ teaspoon ground cumin
- ¼ teaspoon powdered coriander

→ METHOD

To make the peach relish, cover the peaches in boiling water and soak for 30 minutes. Strain and reserve half the liquid. Combine with the rest of the ingredients and simmer for 45 minutes, stirring constantly.

Trim the lamb racks of all fat or have your butcher do it. Put the star anise, soy sauce, 60 ml (2 fl oz) water and mirin into a saucepan, bring to the boil and simmer for 20 minutes, then remove from the heat and cool.

Put the lamb racks in a glass dish and pour the star anise marinade over them, then turn the racks upside down so the meat part is sitting in the marinade. Let them sit there for 30 minutes.

To cook, lift the lamb from the marinade and sit in a roasting tray, meat side up. Brush with the marinade again and cook in a preheated oven at 200ºC until done to your liking. I cook mine for 15–20 minutes – baste the racks with the star anise mixture twice during the cooking. Remove from the oven, lift out the lamb and let rest for 10 minutes before carving, or serve whole if you prefer.

Drain any excess fat from the baking tray and put over high heat. When the sediments start to crackle, pour in the port wine and stir to incorporate. Spoon some over each rack of lamb (or sliced-down lamb) on individual dinner plates. Serve with a spoon of the relish.

VEAL CUTLETS WITH OLIVE, PARSLEY & LIME PESTO
`SERVES 4`

→ INGREDIENTS

- 4 x 200 g (7 oz) veal cutlets
- ¼ teaspoon chopped fresh oregano
- 450 g (16 oz) waxy potatoes, Kipfler or Desiree
- Spray oil
- Salt and ground black pepper

OLIVE, PARSLEY AND LIME PESTO

- 20 green olives, seeds removed
- 2 limes, grated zest only
- 1 lime, juiced
- 2 cloves garlic, peeled and halved
- 1 tablespoon pinenuts, toasted
- 40 g (1.5 oz) flat (Italian) parsley
- 80 ml (2.7 fl oz) extra virgin olive oil

→ METHOD

Trim the veal cutlets if necessary and refrigerate covered with cling wrap until ready to use.

Wash potatoes and peel if desired. Cut into halves or quarters if big and boil in water for 3 minutes. Drain and cool. Refrigerate until ready to use.

Remove veal and potatoes from the refrigerator 10 minutes before use to bring them to room temperature.

Spray the cutlets with plenty of oil and seal on a hot plate by lightly browning both sides. Lower to medium heat to allow to cook to your liking. Sprinkle on some oregano and press onto each cutlet with the back of the cooking spatula. Turn only one more time and repeat the oregano on that side. Sprinkle with salt and pepper on the second turning only.

Spray the potatoes well and cook on a medium-hot plate. Sprinkle with salt and pepper and turn regularly until browned, crisped and cooked through.

When the veal is cooked to your liking, remove and rest for 5 minutes.

To serve, put equal amount of potatoes into the centre of each plate and top with the veal cutlets. Spoon over some of the pesto and serve with cooked broccoli or other green vegetables of your choice.

FOR THE OLIVE, PARSLEY AND LIME PESTO

Put the olives, lime zest, lime juice, garlic, pinenuts and parsley into a food processor bowl and start the motor. Gradually pour in the oil and work to a rough paste. Remove from processor bowl, cover and refrigerate.

STIR-FRIED BEEF & PRAWNS
SERVES 4

The strips of meat that you buy need to be tender so they can be cooked quickly and still remain tender. Sometimes lesser cuts of meat find their way into stir fries and they simply are not suitable. I always buy either the sirloin or the rump and cut it into strips around 1 cm (½ in) thick for use in a dish like this.

→ INGREDIENTS

- 400 g (14 oz) beef strips, of either rump or sirloin
- 60 ml (2 fl oz) soy sauce
- 60 ml (2 fl oz) rice vinegar
- 1 tablespoon peanut or vegetable oil
- 1 medium red chilli, de-seeded and finely chopped
- 1 x 10 cm (4 in) piece lemongrass, finely minced
- 1 tablespoon palm sugar
- 8 king prawns, completely peeled and deveined
- 1 small onion, cut into wedges
- 50 g (1.8 oz) bean shoots
- 8 water chestnuts, finely sliced
- 325 g (11.5 oz) cooked long grain rice
- 50 g (1.8 oz) coriander leaves
- Spray oil

→ METHOD

Make sure the meat is the same size. Add the soy, vinegar, oil, chilli, lemongrass and palm sugar. Mix well and sit covered for 1 hour.

To cook, strain the meat and reserve the soy mixture. Spray the very hot plate liberally with oil and tip on the meat strips immediately. Move around with a spatula. Cook the prawns on an oiled part of the plate and cook the onions on another part of the sprayed plate.

Add in the bean sprouts and water chestnuts and combine all cooking ingredients into a concentrated area on the barbecue.

Spoon over the marinade and lift and toss for another 2 minutes. Lift into a serving bowl, add the coriander and toss together gently. Serve with cooked rice.

VEAL AND HAM BURGERS WITH BEETROOT RELISH

SERVES 4

→ INGREDIENTS

- 4 large bread rolls
- 500 g (35 oz) minced veal
- 250 g (8 oz) minced ham
- 2 eggs
- 1 teaspoon Tabasco sauce
- 1 tablespoon tomato sauce
- 60 g (2 oz) onion, finely diced
- ½ teaspoon salt
- Breadcrumbs, if necessary
- 4 medium-size field mushrooms
- 100 g (3.5 oz) shredded lettuce for the beetroot relish
- 220 g (7 oz) beetroot, cooked, cooled and skins removed
- 2 spring onions, finely minced
- 1 teaspoon anchovy sauce
- 1 tablespoon white wine vinegar
- 2 teaspoons truffle oil, or walnut oil

→ METHOD

Cut the bread rolls in half horizontally and pull out the soft centre of each half to make a well.

Combine the veal, ham, eggs, Tabasco, tomato sauce, onion, salt and the bread removed from the buns, broken into really small pieces. Using your hands, mix well. The bread you have used should be enough to bind the mixture, but if it is too moist, add enough dried breadcrumbs to take up any excess liquid. Shape into four even-sized patties – cover and refrigerate.

Make the relish by grating the beetroot roughly. Combine with the spring onions, anchovy sauce, vinegar and oil and mix well. Leftover relish will keep, refrigerated, for about one week.

Spray the patties with oil and cook on the flat plate on the barbecue over medium heat for one minute.

Spray again, turn and cook the second side for another minute.

Spray the mushrooms on the gill side (the brown underneath part) and cook on the open grill over high heat for two minutes on each side.

Continued over page

VEAL AND HAM BURGERS
WITH BEETROOT RELISH CONTINUED

Lift hamburger patties onto the open grill and cook over high heat for a further three minutes on each side, or until done to your liking. (The time recommended will give you medium-rare patties.)

Spray the insides of the hamburger buns with oil and cook, cut-side-down, on the open grill for 30 seconds. Turn to cook for 30 seconds on the other side.

Lift all ingredients from the barbecue and assemble by putting equal portions of lettuce in the base part of each bread roll. Add a cooked pattie and top with a mushroom.

Spoon beetroot relish on top of the mushrooms and add the top part of the bread roll. Press down to compress the fillings and serve with your choice of salads.

When bread rolls are left flat, fillings can easily slide out as you bite. I adopted the habit of scooping out the centres of the bread rolls after seeing many such disasters. If you make a well on each side, the fillings are held in much better. You can also serve the beetroot relish with cold meats and other barbecued meats.

VENISON SAUSAGES & PARSNIP MASH WITH CUMBERLAND SAUCE

SERVES 4

→ INGREDIENTS

- 400 g (14 oz) parsnips, peeled and core removed
- 100 g (4 oz) Pontiac potatoes, peeled and diced
- 100 g (4 oz) butter
- ½ teaspoon salt

- 8 large venison sausages

FOR THE SAUCE

- 3 tablespoons red currant or quince jelly
- 1 tablespoon English mustard
- ¼ teaspoon ground ginger powder
- 1 teaspoon orange zest, finely grated

→ METHOD

Chop the parsnips to a similar size as the potatoes. Bring to the boil and then simmer until tender. Strain and return to saucepan. Replace the lid and let sit for 3 minutes. Add the butter and mash the two together with the salt. Scoop out into microwave-proof bowl, cover and keep at room temperature.

Make the sauce by combining all ingredients and mix well. Cook in microwave on high for 30 seconds. Remove, mix thoroughly and let sit at room temperature.

Spray the venison sausages with oil and cook on a medium-hot plate. Cooking time will vary according to the size of your sausages. Turn regularly and finish the sausages on the grill for the last couple of minutes of cooking to crisp them up. Remove from barbecue and leave to rest for 2 minutes.

Reheat parsnip mash in the microwave and spoon equal amounts onto individual plates. Lean two sausages onto the mash. Serve the Cumberland Sauce separately with a cooked green vegetable of your choice.

LAMB CUTLETS WITH SOY AND HONEY EGGPLANT

SERVES 4

Lamb cutlets have always been a natural on the barbecue. Served in racks of several cutlets, they became fashionable in restaurants in the '80s. In this recipe they are cooked quickly over high heat so that they remain succulent and pink in the centre.

→ INGREDIENTS

- 4 banana eggplants (aubergines), about 90 g (2 oz) each
- 2 tablespoon dark soy sauce
- 2 tablespoon light olive oil
- 1 tablespoon honey
- ½ teaspoon freshly ground black pepper
- 12 trimmed lamb cutlets, each 2 cm (3/4 in) thick
- 1 teaspoon salt

→ METHOD

Top and tail the eggplant and slice in half lengthwise. Score the flesh by making diagonal cuts to form diamond shapes, being careful not the cut through the skin.

Mix the soy, oil, honey and pepper.

Brush soy mixture on the cut side of the eggplant halves, ensuring that some mixture penetrates down into the scored flesh.

Spray the flat plate with oil and cook eggplant halves, cut side down for two minutes. Turn and cook for a further minute.

At the same time, cook cutlets on the open grill for 2 minutes on each side, sprinkling them with salt as you turn them.

Place 2 eggplant halves, cut side up on each plate. Stack 3 lamb cutlets adjacent to the eggplant and serve with salads of your choice.

CLASSIC RISSOLES

Rissoles come in many shapes, sizes and variations, but I have never served them without someone at the table screaming, 'Rissoles – I love 'em!' They remain a perennial favourite.

→ INGREDIENTS

- 2 tablespoons vegetable oil
- 1 tablespoon butter
- 1 small onion, finely chopped
- 125 g (4 oz) rolled oats
- 750 g (26 oz) beef, finely minced
- 2 tablespoons tomato sauce
- ½ teaspoon Tabasco sauce

- 2 large eggs, beaten lightly
- ½ teaspoon salt
- 1 teaspoon freshly ground black pepper
- 8 medium size shiitake mushrooms, stems removed
- Lemon and mustard butter (see page 22)

→ METHOD

Heat oil and butter in a pan until foaming and fry onions gently for two minutes. Tip onion into a large bowl and add rolled oats, beef, tomato sauce, Tabasco, eggs, salt and pepper. Using your hands, mix well. Refrigerate mixture for one hour. With wet hands, shape mixture into eight patties, each about 2.5cm (1in) thick, and put onto plate.

Spray the flat plate with oil and cook rissoles for one minute, then spray the rissoles with oil, turn over and cook on second side for another minute. Flip them onto the open grill and cook for a further two minutes on each side, or until done to your liking. Cooking time will vary with the thickness of the rissoles.

Meanwhile, spray mushrooms with oil on the gill side (the brown underneath part) first and cook, turning regularly, on the open grill for the same time as the rissoles.

Place two rissoles on each plate and top each with a mushroom. Serve with a little lemon and mustard butter and a salad of your choice.

LOIN OF LAMB WITH ROMA TOMATOES AND BUTTERNUT PUMPKIN

SERVES 4

Butternut pumpkin is a perfect partner for lamb. This member of the squash family is remarkably versatile – try it in pickles or, mashed, as the basis for soufflés and scones. Roma tomatoes, sometimes called egg tomatoes, are superb for both their flavour and structure.

→INGREDIENTS

- 500 g (18 oz) boneless loin of lamb, cut into four steaks
- 2 tablespoons extra virgin olive oil
- 2 parsnips, each about 220 g (7 oz)
- 2 Roma tomatoes, cut in half lengthwise
- ¼ teaspoon salt
- 1 butternut pumpkin, about 750 g (24 oz)
- Balsamic vinegar

→METHOD

Trim lamb steaks, place in a bowl and pour olive oil over to coat.

Peel parsnips and cut off any of the fibrous end pieces. Cut each into four wedges and remove the woody core. Sprinkle the cut side of the tomatoes with salt.

Cut the pumpkin in half lengthwise. Cover one half with plastic wrap and refrigerate for another use. Cook remaining half, with seeds still in, in the microwave for 7 minutes.

Spray the cut side of the pumpkin with oil and cook on the open grill over high heat for 5 minutes. Turn over and leave to cook for 10 minutes. Scoop out the seeds at this stage with a spoon, taking care, as the pumpkin will be hot.

Spray parsnips with oil and cook on the open grill over high heat for four minutes. Lift parsnip onto the flat plate and cook over a medium heat for a further 4 minutes, turning regularly. Turn over the pumpkin again and leave to cook for 10 minutes.

Spray cut side of the tomato halves with oil and cook, cut side down, on the flat plate for 2 minutes. Turn and cook for 2 minutes more.

Cook oiled lamb steaks on the flat plate over medium heat for 4 minutes on each side. Rest for 4 minutes before slicing and serving with the vegetables and balsamic vinegar.

PORK CHOPS WITH BLUE CHEESE MAYO & SWEETCORN POTATO CAKES

SERVES 4

→ INGREDIENTS

- 4–8 pork chops, depending on size
- 120 g (4 oz) blue cheese of your choice, crumbled
- 1 tablespoon white vinegar
- 1 tablespoon spring onion, finely chopped
- 240 ml (8 fl oz) mayonnaise
- 400 g (14 oz) mashed potatoes, at room temperature
- 4 tablespoons canned corn kernels, drained
- 1 egg, beaten
- Salt and white pepper to taste
- Dry breadcrumbs
- Spray oil

→ METHOD

Trim the pork chops of the rind if you like. Set to one side.

Whisk the cheese and vinegar until the combined, stir in the onion and fold in the mayonnaise.

Make the potato cakes by mixing the potatoes, corn, egg and salt and pepper together. Add enough breadcrumbs to take up the moisture and to make a firm mixture. Evenly divide the potato mixture and shape into patties. Refrigerate if not using immediately.

Cook the chops on a hot plate and when nearly done, move to the hot grill plate to complete the cooking. Leave on the plate if thick and reduce heat to cook through.

Spray the potato cakes until lightly browned on each side of the hot plate.

Serve cakes with the pork chops; spoon sauce over the chops or serve on the side. Freshly steamed broccoli completes this dish.

DUCK QUESADILLAS & SEMI-ROASTED TOMATO SALSA
SERVES 4

→ INGREDIENTS

- 750 g (26 oz) boneless duck breasts
- 40 g (1.5 oz) sliced jalapeno chillies
- ¼ onion, finely chopped
- 12 g (0.5 oz) coriander leaves, rinsed and ripped
- Salt to taste
- 120 g (4 oz) cheddar cheese, grated
- 8 medium flour tortillas
- Semi-roasted Tomato Salsa (see recipe below)

SEMI-ROASTED TOMATO SALSA

- 170 g (6 oz) semi-roasted tomatoes, roughly chopped
- 40 g (1.5 oz) red onion, peeled and finely chopped
- 1 tablespoon Jalapeno chillies, minced
- ½ tablespoon brown sugar
- 1 tablespoon brown vinegar
- 2 tablespoons olive oil

→ METHOD

Make this delicious salsa at least four hours before use by mixing all the ingredients together – it will store in the refrigerator for five days.

Trim the duck breasts of as much fat as possible. Leave the skin on and cut two diagonal slashes into the skin to let the fat escape during cooking.

Mix the chillies, onion, coriander leaves and salt together to make the chilli mix.

Put the duck on a medium-hot plate, skin-side down. Allow to cook and to brown very well, about 3 minutes then turn and cook for 5–7 minutes. Flip over onto a medium-hot grill to cook on the skin side for 2 minutes or until medium. Remove and let rest for 5 minutes. Slice into very thin strips when cool enough to handle.

Lay a flour tortilla out and spoon cheese over half of it. Top with some duck slices and then some of the chilli mix. Fold the empty half over the stuffing and tuck the folding edge in under some of the filling. Put to one side and repeat until all tortillas are filled.

Spray a medium-hot plate with oil and add the quesadillas, cheese-side-down first. Allow to cook for 1–2 minutes. Spray the top with oil and flip over quickly, the cheese should have melted enough to grip most of the filling. Serve with the salsa in a separate bowl.

CHICKEN FAJITAS
SERVES 4

→ INGREDIENTS

- 500 g (18 oz) chicken breast meat, boneless and skinless
- 1 tablespoon corn oil
- 1 tablespoon sherry vinegar
- 1 tablespoon allspice, ground
- ½ tablespoon oregano, dried & ground
- 2 tablespoons onion flakes, pre-cooked
- 1 teaspoon salt
- ¼ teaspoon chilli powder
- Spray oil
- 100 g (3.5 oz) lettuce, shredded
- 50 g (1.8 oz) carrot, grated
- 2 medium salad tomatoes, cut into wedges
- 120 ml (4 fl oz) sour cream
- 8 wheat flour tortillas

→ METHOD

Cut the chicken breast across the grain into 1cm (0.4 in) wide strips and place in bowl.

Mix the oil, vinegar, sherry, allspice, oregano, onion flakes, salt, and chilli powder and pour over the chicken. Stir to coat the pieces, then cover and refrigerate for at least 2 hours.

Liberally spray a hot plate with oil and tip on the chicken strips. Spread over the plate with a spatula and cook by tossing and lifting the pieces and allowing them to brown for about 5 minutes.

Spray the tortillas with oil and heat very quickly on the grill. They take about 15–30 seconds on each side. Stack on plate to keep warm and cover with foil if you like.

Lift the chicken onto a large platter and serve with heaped lettuce, carrot and tomatoes on another platter.

Serve the chicken, salad items, tortillas and sour cream in the centre of the table for people to share.

CHICKEN BREAST SALTIMBOCCA
SERVES 4

→ INGREDIENTS

- 4 x 150 g (5 oz) chicken breasts, boneless and skinless
- Spray oil
- 4 good slices ham, cut in half or enough to cover the chicken
- 8 sage leaves
- 4 slices mozzarella cheese or enough to cover the chicken

→ METHOD

Put the single chicken breasts in between clingwrap and pound gently with a cooking mallet until evenly flat.

Spray the breasts with oil and seal each breast (for 30 seconds on each side) on a hot plate. Do not cook through as you have another cooking process to do yet and overcooking will dry out the chicken. Lift onto baking tray.

Cover each breast with ham and two sage leaves and cover with cheese. Sit tray on cake cooling rack and sit on plate (do not have burners on under the plate but the two burners of the grill going at high heat)–lower lid and cook until the cheese melts and is bubbling.

Serve on bed of cooked vegetables or pasta of your choice.

CHICKEN BREAST WITH TZATZIKI AND GREEK SALAD
MAKES 4

→ INGREDIENTS

- 4 x 155g (5oz) chicken breast, skin on
- 2 tablespoons extra virgin olive oil
- for the tzatziki
- 1 Lebanese or telegraph cucumber, about 25cm (10in) long
- 1 teaspoon salt
- 2 cloves garlic, peeled and crushed
- 375ml (12fl oz) plain thick yoghurt
- 1 tablespoon dried mint
- 1 tablespoon extra virgin olive oil

- for the greek salad
- 1 medium-size head iceberg lettuce, washed and crisped
- 2 medium-size tomatoes, cut into wedges
- 125g (4oz) fetta cheese, diced
- 20 Kalamata olives
- 2 tablespoons lemon juice
- 1 tablespoon extra virgin olive oil

→ METHOD

Trim the chicken breast and soak in olive oil.

To make the tzatziki, cut the cucumber in half lengthwise. Using a teaspoon, scoop out and discard seeds. Peel each half and slice into very fine half-moon shapes. Place in a bowl, sprinkle with salt and tumble. Leave for one hour. Rinse cucumber under cold water and drain of paper towels. Pat as dry as possible and place in a serving bowl. Add garlic, yoghurt, mint and olive oil and stir well. Refrigerate for at least one hour before serving.

For the salad, break the crisped lettuce into bite-size pieces in a salad bowl. Add tomatoes and add cheese and olives. Cover and refrigerate.

Place chicken, skin-side-down, on the flat plate and cook for two minutes. Drizzle chicken with a little of the oil it was soaking in. Turn over and cook for a further two minutes. Put onto an open grill and cook for two minutes skin side up. Turn over and cook for two minutes.

Remove the chicken from the barbecue onto paper towel. Leave in a warm place to rest the chicken for about four minutes before serving.

Spoon some tzatziki on one side of each plate. Slice the chicken across the grain into rounds and arrange in a fan around the tzatziki. Drizzle combined lemon juice and olive oil over the salad and toss well.

Poultry

CHAR GRILLED DUCK BREASTS AND CURRIED CHICKPEAS
`SERVES 6`

→ INGREDIENTS

- 4 x 250 g (8 oz) Muscovy duck breasts
- Curried chickpeas (see recipe on page 155)
- 2 tablespoons rice vinegar
- ½ tablespoon cooking salt
- 1 tablespoon Sumac

→ METHOD

Slash the skin side of the breasts to allow the fat to escape during cooking and have the curried chickpeas ready for reheating.

Rub the vinegar into the skin side of the duck breast. Lay them over the high heat part of the open slats, skin side down and leave there for 1–2 minutes. Watch the breast carefully as flames can scorch the skin, rather than brown it. Sprinkle the flesh side of the breasts with a little salt and half the sumac and turn over. Sprinkle the skin sides with the remaining salt and Sumac and leave to cook for 1 minute. Turn the breast back onto their skin sides and move to a part of the open slats where the temperature is medium. Leave to cook for a further 2–3 minutes. Turn breasts over and cook on the flesh side until done, 5–7 minutes. By now, the skin should be crispy and browned. Remove from the barbecue when done and let rest for at least 10 minutes before slicing.

Serve on a bed of curried chickpeas.

CHAR-ROASTED CHICKEN WITH OLD-FASHIONED BREAD STUFFING

SERVES 4

Small meat thermometers are inexpensive and so helpful in letting you know the internal temperature of the item being cooked. For the chicken, test (insert thermometer) between the thigh and the body of the bird. Also test the centre of the stuffing. If you have too much stuffing, put it into the neck cavity of the chicken and secure by wrapping the skin around the stuffing and skewer into place.

→ INGREDIENTS

- 1 kg (35 oz) free range chicken
- Spray olive oil
- Salt

BREAD STUFFING

- 150 g (5 oz) day-old bread, broken into small pieces (I leave the crust on)
- 60 g (2 oz) onion, finely diced

- 1 tablespoon each parsley, rosemary and thyme, roughly chopped
- 1 teaspoon nutmeg, freshly grated
- Zest of one orange
- 1 egg
- 2 tablespoons oil (I used macadamia because I like that nutty essence)

→ METHOD

Preheat barbecue to 180–200°C. Have a maximum of only two burners on at one time.

Wipe out the inside of chicken. Mix all the stuffing ingredients together. Put inside the gut cavity and push firmly. Do not overfill as it will burst out during cooking. Tie or skewer the legs around the opening and spray with oil.

Put into an aluminium roasting tray or sit on a cake cooling rack (or you can use a rotisserie or the roasting tray that hangs from the lid). Sprinkle with salt and cook for 50 minutes. Baste twice and turn to ensure even cooking.

Internal temperature of chicken must be at least 75°C. Use a small meat thermometer. Remove from barbecue, rest for 5 minutes and cut into quarters to serve with vegetables or salad.

DUCK BREASTS WITH BOK CHOY & CELERIAC SALAD

SERVES 4

The cooking of the duck breast is dependent entirely upon the depth of flesh. If you are unable to get Muscovy duck breasts, you will more than likely end up with quite thin flesh. Muscovy duck breasts have an excellent depth of flesh, generally around 2-3cm (1in) thick and sometimes larger. The cooking time that I have recommended will bring the duck breasts out to medium to rare so you will need to cook them longer if you prefer well done – which I would heartily discourage.

→ INGREDIENTS

- 4 x 120 g (4 oz) duck breast, Muscovy is the best
- 200 g (7 oz) celeriac, peeled and roughly grated
- 2 medium eschallots, peeled and finely diced
- 1 tablespoon Japanese pickle ginger, finely sliced
- 120 ml (4 fl oz) mayonnaise
- 1 tablespoon pickled ginger juice
- 4 medium bok choy, trimmed, washed and halved

→ METHOD

Trim the duck breasts if necessary and cut two slashes into the skin.

Combine the celeriac, eschallots, ginger, mayonnaise and ginger juice. Stir well and cover to refrigerate for 1 hour before use.

Take the duck from the refrigerator 10 minutes before use; place it onto a hot grill, skin-side down and cook for 2 minutes. Do not move the duck as you are looking for really good crisp marks on the skin. Turn the duck breast onto where it has already been cooking so that the natural fat that is on the grill will be used for the bare flesh and stop sticking.

Cook for 4 minutes, remove from heat and allow to sit for 5 minutes before slicing.

Place the bok choy on a medium hot plate and cook for 1–1½ minutes, turning only the once; the time will vary depending on the thickness of the white part of the bok choy as it must be crunchy.

Place two halves of the bok choy in the centre of the plate, spoon over equal amounts of the salad. Slice the duck breast into rounds and place on top of the celeriac salad.

CHICKEN WITH CORN AND MANGO SALSA

SERVES 4

→ INGREDIENTS

FOR THE CHICKEN

- 400 g (14 oz) cooked skinless, boneless chicken breast
- 100 g (3.5 oz) mixed baby lettuce leaves
- 20 cooked asparagus tips
- 200 g (7 oz) cooked unpeeled potatoes, diced

FOR THE SALSA

- 150 g (5.5 oz) mango flesh, diced
- 150 g (5.5 oz) corn kernels, canned or bottled
- 1 very small red onion, finely diced
- 1 small banana chilli, deseeded and minced
- 1 tablespoon coriander, chopped
- Salt and ground black pepper to taste
- 3 tablespoons apple cider vinegar
- 1 tablespoon mustard seed oil

→ METHOD

Cut the chicken meat into bite-sized pieces and set to one side.

Divide the lettuce leaves onto four plates. Top with equal amounts of asparagus, potatoes and chicken.

Make the salsa by combining all ingredients and stirring well. Spoon the salsa over the salad ingredients and serve immediately.

I must confess that I use very little salt anymore and have adjusted to the taste of natural, flavoursome foods. Every now and then I do have a little salt, but it is up to you if you use it or not. My mum hardly ever used salt on our tasty homegrown veggies in my childhood. She maintains that if you don't get used to it as a child you won't ever – some homegrown philosophy.

CHICKEN AND MUSHROOM MOUSSAKA

This version of the brilliant Greek dish would more than likely spark a revolution were it seen in Greece. I have loved moussaka for years and am determined to eat it... even if very low in fat but high in flavour.

→ INGREDIENTS

- 60 ml (2 fl oz) salt-reduced chicken stock
- 1 medium onion, finely chopped
- 1 small carrot, peeled and grated
- 400 g (14 oz) lean chicken mince
- Spray olive oil
- 6 medium mushrooms, stems removed
- 2 medium-size eggplants (aubergines), thinly sliced lengthwise
- 160 g (5.5 oz) salt-reduced, no added sugar, crushed tomatoes
- 360 ml (12 fl oz) no-fat plain yoghurt
- 1 large free-range egg
- 120 g (4 oz) fat-free cheese, grated

→ METHOD

Preheat oven 180ºC. Heat stock to boiling, quickly cook onion and carrot, add the mince and mash to stop it forming lumps. Cook for 5 minutes then cool.

Spray mushrooms with a film of oil, cook under preheated grill for 2 minutes on a tray and cool.

Spoon half the cooled meat mixture into a suitable ovenproof dish. Layer in the mushrooms and top with eggplant. Add the rest of the meat. Now spoon the tomatoes over the top of the mixture – sprinkle with ground black pepper to taste.

Mix the yoghurt and egg then spoon evenly over all ingredients. Sprinkle with the cheese and bake in the oven for 40 minutes or until the top is golden brown.

Serve hot or at room temperature with green vegetables of your choice or lemon-dressed green salad.

I have found that when the eggplants are medium to small they do not need the 'salt leaching' process. This moussaka produces quite a lot of liquid, which I spoon over as I serve. Alternatively, you can drain the juices, but they are so good.

QUAIL & PINEAPPLE SCENTED COUS COUS
SERVES 4

→ INGREDIENTS

- 4 large quails
- Olive oil
- 4 x 2 cm (0.8 in) thick slices fresh pineapple, core removed and cut in large dices
- 1 small red onion, finely chopped
- 200 g (7 oz) dried cous cous
- 300 ml (10 fl oz) boiling water
- 1 tablespoon extra virgin olive oil
- 1 teaspoon Baharat spice
- 15 g (0.5 oz) basil leaves, ripped
- 15 g (0.5 oz) mint leaves, ripped
- Salt and powdered black pepper
- 2 tablespoons toasted sesame seeds

→ METHOD

Cut the quails into quarters and remove the winglets. Put into a bowl and drizzle over some oil. Toss to coat the quail and refrigerate until ready for use.

Rehydrate cous cous by pouring on boiling water in a large bowl. Leave to sit for 30 seconds, then then add diced onion and extra virgin olive oil. Fork through to stop the grains sticking together.

Remove the quail from the refrigerator 10 minutes before use. Drain the quarters of the oil and cook on a medium-hot plate. Turn regularly until done – quail is best not over-cooked.

Flash cook the pineapple on a very hot plate so the dices are lightly browned. Remove and toss with the Baharat and salt and pepper. Add to the cous cous with the herbs and mix thoroughly.

Serve the cous cous with the pineapple and quail on top.

CHICKEN CHOI BAO
MAKES 4

→ INGREDIENTS

- 500 g (18 oz) chicken, minced
- 1 tablespoon vegetable oil
- 1 small brown onion, finely chopped
- 4 cloves garlic, peeled and finely chopped
- 60 ml (2 fl oz) hoi sin sauce
- 100 g (3.5 oz) water chestnuts, drained and roughly chopped
- 1 small bunch fresh coriander, leaves only and finely broken
- 8 medium size lettuce cups, washed and crisped
- Cooked brown or basmati rice

FOR THE SAUCE

- 2 tablespoons rice vinegar
- 3 tablespoons Tamari light soy sauce
- 1 small red chilli, seeds in and minced

→ METHOD

Check the chicken to ensure all fat is removed.

Bring the oil to smoking point over high heat and add the onion and garlic. Stir and add the chicken mince. Use the back of a large spoon or a wok spatula to mash the meat so it does not go lumpy. Pour in the hoi sin and add the water chestnuts. Cook for 10 minutes stirring occasionally.

Make the sauce by combining all ingredients.

Stir the coriander into the chicken and serve in a large bowl in the middle of the table with the lettuce cups and sauce to one side. Boiled, long grain rice always sets off this dish. I generally use brown rice but basmati is fine.

You can substitute the rice vinegar with regular white vinegar.

CHICKEN, WILTED SPINACH AND CURRIED CHICKPEAS

→ INGREDIENTS

- 4 x 125 g (4.5 oz) skinless chicken breasts, cut into medallions
- 2 spring onions, chopped
- 1 tablespoon linseed oil
- ½ medium onion, finely chopped
- ½ medium carrot, finely chopped
- 2 tablespoons Indian curry powder
- 400 g (14 oz) canned pre-cooked chickpeas, drained
- 480 ml (16 fl oz) water
- 200 g (7 oz) baby spinach leaves

→ METHOD

Ensure all fat is removed from the chicken medallions. Heat enough water to poach the chicken, add chicken and spring onion and simmer for 10 minutes. Turn off the heat until ready to use.

Heat linseed oil and lightly fry the onion and carrot pieces. Tip in the curry powder and stir. Add the drained chickpeas and stir to coat with the curry mixture. Pour in the water, bring to the boil then reduce to a simmer and cook for 30 minutes. You may need more water, depending on the saucepan you use.

Reheat the poaching stock, simmer the chicken slices to cook through: around 3–5 minutes. Do this in batches, depending on your pan size. Keep slices warm if this is the case.

In another saucepan bring 60 ml (2 fl oz) chicken poaching liquid to the boil. Tip in the spinach and stir to allow it to wilt/break down. Do not overcook or you will lose the colour and nutritional value. Drain well and keep warm.

Serve by putting equal amounts of chickpeas into the centre of four deep-welled plates. Top with spinach, then equal amounts of chicken slices. Spoon over some of the chicken poaching liquid and serve immediately. Serve with good bread.

This delicious chickpea recipe is best made the day before, to let the flavour meld. I often buy larger chicken breasts for this recipe and cut them into medallions for easier cooking.

TURKEY SAN CHOY BAO
SERVES 4

This versatile Asian dish has so many variations – this is just one. It makes a great starter course. The constant is that it is best served in the middle of the table for all to help themselves, which is communal and gets your guests talking to each other. Oh, and it tastes just great!

→ INGREDIENTS

- 1 large iceberg lettuce
- ½ tablespoon light olive oil
- 400 g (14 oz) turkey mince
- 4 white spring onions, finely minced; reserve tops
- 2 tablespoons salt-reduced soy sauce
- 1 teaspoon five-spice powder
- 1 tablespoon cornflour
- 60 ml (2 fl oz) salt-reduced chicken stock
- 200 g (7 oz) canned water chestnuts, drained, sliced
- 1 large fruity red chilli, sliced into rounds
- 650 g (23 oz) cooked Doongara rice or another low-GI rice

→ METHOD

Remove the core out of the lettuce and run water into it to wash and help separate the leaves. Take eight larger outside leaves and trim. Shake off excess water and crisp in the refrigerator. Reserve the remainder of the lettuce for salads or sandwiches.

Heat oil over high heat in a wok and add the turkey mince, spring onion, soy sauce and five spice powder – mash with the back of a spoon or a potato masher to avoid large lumps forming. Cook until browned.

Mix the cornflour with the stock and stir into the meat with the water chestnuts. Cook for a further 3 minutes as you stir to allow the dish to thicken.

Spoon equal amounts of the mixture into the chilled lettuce leaves and top with chilli. Shred some green tops from the spring onion to sprinkle over as well. Serve with steamed Chinese green vegetables and the cooked Doongara rice.

If you want to serve this dish as a starter, you would not have the cooked green vegetables with it, and you should only cook half the quantity of rice.

TURKEY AND FETA TORTILLAS
SERVES 4

→ INGREDIENTS

- 8 flat corn tortillas
- 100 g (3.5 oz) shredded lettuce
- 2 green spring onions, trimmed and roughly chopped
- 300 g (10 oz) cooked lean turkey breast, sliced
- 2 roma/egg tomatoes, trimmed and sliced lengthwise
- 150 g (5 oz) reduced-fat feta cheese, diced or roughly crumbled
- 2 large green chillies, seeds removed, cut into fine strips
- 25 g (0.9 oz) coriander leaves
- 4 lemon wedges

→ METHOD

Warm the tortillas by passing over a gas flame constantly on the barbecue grill or by leaving in a very hot oven for 30 seconds. Lay out on bench and assemble immediately.

Evenly distribute the ingredients on one half of each tortilla. Put the lettuce down first, sprinkle over the spring onions, add the sliced turkey, tomatoes, cheese, chilli and coriander. Fold the naked half of the tortilla over the filling and serve with a lemon wedge on the side.

This is ideal for lunch. Serve with a dessert or seasonal fruit after you have devoured the scrummy tortillas.

TURKEY MINCE BOLOGNAISE AND SPAGHETTI

SERVES 4

→ INGREDIENTS

- 360 ml (12 fl oz) salt-reduced beef or chicken stock
- 90 g (3 oz) onion, chopped
- 90 g (3 oz) carrots, peeled and chopped
- 90 g (3 oz) celery, chopped
- 3 cloves garlic, minced
- 400 g (14 oz) turkey meat, minced
- 1 teaspoon ground nutmeg
- 120ml (4 fl oz) red wine
- 300 g (10 oz) tomatoes, salt-reduced, no added sugar, crushed
- 2 bay leaves
- 1 tablespoon dried oregano
- 250 g (9 oz) dried wholemeal spaghetti
- 25 g (0.9 oz) parsley, chopped

→ METHOD

Put half a cup of the stock with the onion, carrots, celery and garlic into a largish pot and simmer for 2 minutes. Add the turkey and mash with a potato masher to stop lumps forming, stirring as you go.

Sprinkle in nutmeg and stir as you pour in the wine. Tip in tomatoes and remaining stock; add bay leaves and oregano and simmer for 50–60 minutes. This dish can be quite wet and the longer you simmer it, the more the liquid evaporates and concentrates flavours.

Cook the pasta in lots of boiling unsalted water – strain and top with equal amounts of the meat sauce. Sprinkle parsley over as you serve. A good salad or cooked greens like broccolini balance out this meal. Also, good bread must be served with this dish.

This is one of many different recipes for bolognaise sauce for pasta and one of my favourites as the turkey meat is low in fat and high in flavour. It is best made the day before use – this allows any fat to settle to the top and be removed when firm. It also lets the flavours meld.

LIME CHICKEN AND GINGER PUMPKIN BARLEY

SERVES 4

→ INGREDIENTS

FOR THE BARLEY

- 90 g (3 oz) onion, finely chopped
- 30 g (1 oz) green ginger, cut into slivers
- 215 g (7.5 oz) pearl barley
- 720 ml (24 fl oz) salt-reduced chicken stock
- 200 g (7 oz) blue pumpkin, peeled, cut into 2cm (0.8 in) dices
- 1 red capsicum (pepper), finely diced

FOR THE CHICKEN

- 500 g (17.5 oz) boneless chicken breast
- 1 large lime (finely grated zest and juice)
- 1 large kaffir lime leaf
- Spray oil

→ METHOD

Preheat oven to 180ºC. Put the onion, ginger, barley and chicken stock into a suitable pot and bring to the boil; stir, reduce to a simmer and put the lid on the saucepan to cook for 20 minutes.

Cut the chicken into medallions and cover with the zest and lime juice. Cut the de-ribbed kaffir leaf into really fine strips and add to the chicken with ground black pepper to taste. Toss to coat the chicken; leave to sit for 10 minutes only.

Back to the barley: stir in the diced pumpkin and capsicum, put the lid on and cook for a further 20–30 minutes or until the barley is soft. Check on the liquid level: you may need to add more stock.

Mist oil onto a baking-paper-lined oven tray and put the chicken medallions onto it. Cook for 10 minutes or until cooked through but not overdone.

Spoon the barley into the centre of individual bowls. Top with equal amounts of chicken and serve with a rocket and green bean salad dressed with lemon juice and ground black pepper.

I use pearl barley a lot and it is just delicious. If you can find the whole barley, do buy it; but remember that it will take longer to cook as it has more husk layers.

SALT AND PEPPER QUAIL WITH WILTED SPINACH AND PLUM SAUCE

`SERVES 4`

Quails cook very quickly on the barbecue, and like all game, are best served rare to medium-rare, because with further cooking, the meat tends to dry out and lose flavour and texture.

→ INGREDIENTS

- 8 quails
- 1 tablespoon table salt
- 2 teaspoons white pepper
- 2 teaspoons caster sugar
- 1 teaspoon allspice

- 1 tablespoon peanut oil
- 220 g (7 oz) spinach, washed and stems removed
- 60 ml (2 fl oz) Asian plum sauce

→ METHOD

Halve each quail by first cutting through the backbone and then through the breastbone. Combine salt, pepper, sugar and allspice and mix well. Spray quail halves with oil and cook, skin side down, on the open grill for 2–3 minutes. Spray cut side of the quails, turn over and cook for a further 3 minutes.

Lift from the barbecue and dredge both sides with the salt mixture. Shake off excess salt and pepper and return to the kitchen.

Heat a wok over high heat and pour in the peanut oil. When it starts to smoke, drop spinach into the wok and stir immediately with tongs. Cook for 3–4 minutes. The spinach will rapidly decrease in volume as it cooks.

Serve quails and spinach on individual plates with plum sauce on the side and boiled rice.

CHICKEN & LIME MARINADE WITH PEANUT SAUCE

→ INGREDIENTS

- 8 chicken thighs, total of 1 kg (35 oz), trimmed of all fat
- 120 ml (4 fl oz) lime juice, fresh
- 1 tablespoon ginger, minced
- 3 kaffir lime leaves, rib removed and finely shredded
- 1 green chilli, large, seeded and chopped
- 1 tablespoon sugar
- 2 x 120 ml (4 fl oz) peanut sauce (see recipe below)
- 1 tablespoon peanut oil
- 8 sprigs coriander
- Spray oil

PEANUT SAUCE

- 6 tablespoons peanut butter (smooth or crunchy)
- 240 ml (8 fl oz) water
- 1 clove garlic
- 2 teaspoons palm sugar
- 1 red chilli, de-seeded and roughly chopped
- 2 tablespoons soy sauce, light
- 1 tablespoon lemon juice
- 1 tablespoon fish sauce
- 120 ml (4 fl oz) coconut milk

→ METHOD

FOR THE PEANUT SAUCE

Put peanut butter and water in a saucepan and stir over moderate heat until mixed. Remove from heat and add all other ingredients. Return to moderate heat and stir for 5 minutes.

Cut the chicken thighs in half so you have 16 pieces.

Mix the lime juice, ginger, lime leaves, chilli and sugar. Pour onto the chicken thighs and move the meat through the marinade so it coats evenly. Refrigerate for 30 minutes.

Spray medium-hot plate and add the chicken thighs which have been drained from the marinade and cook the chicken for 2 minutes on each side, adding a little of the remaining marinade, if any.

With a sharp knife and a set of tongs, cut the chicken thighs into strips about 1cm (0.4in) wide. Bring all the chicken pieces to a concentrated area on the plate and pour over 120 ml (4 fl oz) peanut sauce. Cook and coat with sauce until done. Lift the chicken onto a serving plate and pour over the other half cup of peanut sauce to serve.

BARBECUE CHICKEN BREAST WITH PARSLEY SALAD
SERVES 4

There is no doubting the versatility of chicken in all areas of cooking and this recipe is simplicity itself!

→ INGREDIENTS

- 4 x 155 g (5 oz) chicken breasts, skin left on

PARSLEY SALAD

- 155 g (5 oz) curly parsley, washed and roughly chopped
- 10 basil leaves
- 60 g (2 oz) peanuts, roasted and crushed
- 1 large green capsicum (pepper)
- 2 green onions, roughly chopped
- 30 g (1 oz) raw sugar
- 2 tablespoons nam pla (fish sauce)
- 2 tablespoons peanut oil
- 1 tablespoon rice vinegar

→ METHOD

Butterfly the chicken breast by slicing through the thick part of each breast, taking care not to slice through completely. Open out so that you have a butterfly shaped piece of meat.

Make the salad by combining the parsley, basil, peanuts, capsicum and green onion. Combine the sugar, fish sauce, oil and vinegar and mix well until sugar is dissolved.

Add dressing to salad and toss well. Cover and refrigerate.

Spray the cut side of the chicken and cook on the flat plate for one minute. Spray the uncut side with oil, flip the chicken breast over and cook the second side for another minute.

Lift the chicken breast onto the open grill and cook for a further 1 ½ minutes on each side. Remove the chicken breast, drain on paper towel and return to the kitchen.

Cut chicken breasts into halves along the existing lines so that you have 8 pieces of chicken of similar size.

Place 2 pieces of chicken on the centre of each plate to form a 'V'. Spoon some parsley salad into the 'V' and serve.

SEAFOOD

SWORDFISH KEBABS WITH MANGO & LYCHEE SALSA
SERVES 4

I try to use stainless steel skewers as they conduct some heat through to the middle of fish pieces so they cook evenly.

→ INGREDIENTS

- 600 g (20 oz) swordfish fillets, not broadbill swordfish
- 1 tablespoon sesame seeds
- ½ tablespoon sesame oil
- 1 tablespoon rice oil
- 60 ml (2 fl oz) soy sauce
- 230 g (8 oz) mango flesh, diced
- 115 g (4 oz) lychees, deseeded and diced

- 15 g (0.5 oz) green spring onions, finely diced
- 60 ml (2 fl oz) lime juice
- 8 coriander leaves, roughly chopped
- 1 teaspoon fish sauce
- 1 large green fruity chilli, minced
- Coriander leaves for decoration

→ METHOD

Cut the swordfish into even pieces. Thread equal quantities onto oiled stainless steel skewers. Refrigerate until ready for use.

Make the sesame baste by pounding the seeds in a mortar and pestle and, when crushed, adding the oils and soy. Mix well and set to one side.

Make the salsa by combining the mango, lychees, green spring onion, lime juice, coriander, fish sauce and chilli. Gently toss. Refrigerate until ready for use.

Brush the swordfish kebabs with the sesame baste and place onto medium-hot plate. Turn regularly and carefully and baste as you go. Cook until just done because the fish cooks on when it has left the barbecue.

Spoon salsa into the middle of individual plates, top with swordfish and decorate with plenty of coriander leaves.

PRAWNS WITH LAKSA
SERVES 4

Rice vermicelli noodles are easy to make because you simply soak them in boiling water for 5–10 minutes then drain.

→ INGREDIENTS

- 24 large green king prawns
- Spray vegetable oil

LAKSA

- 3 x 10cm (4 in) stalks lemongrass, white part only and roughly chopped
- 3cm (1in) galangal, peeled and roughly chopped
- 3cm (1in) green ginger root, peeled and roughly chopped
- 2 small red chillies, seeds in and roughly chopped
- 2 tablespoons vegetable oil
- 1 tablespoon yellow curry powder
- 1 teaspoon chilli sauce or to taste
- 2 teaspoons tamarind paste
- 360 ml (12 fl oz) coconut milk
- ½ tablespoon fish sauce
- Ground white pepper and white sugar to taste
- 2 tablespoons lightly browned desiccated coconut
- 250 g (9 oz) cooked vermicelli noodles
- Garnish with 2 sliced eschalots, 1 sliced lime, 1 shredded small Lebanese cucumber and 50 g (1.8 oz) Vietnamese mint leaves

→ METHOD

Completely peel and de-vein prawns and make a stock using heads and shells with 720 ml (24 fl oz) water; simmer to reduce to 240 ml (8 fl oz). Barbecue prawns by spraying with oil and cooking on a hot grill.

Put the lemongrass, galangal, ginger and chillies into a food processor and work into a paste (you may need to add a little water) or you can use a mortar and pestle.

Heat oil in a wok and fry lemongrass paste mixture for 2 minutes; add the prawn stock, curry powder, chilli sauce and tamarind puree and bring to a simmer to cook for 2 minutes. Pour in the coconut milk, season to taste with fish sauce.

Add the desiccated coconut to the coconut sauce mix to thicken it; simmer for 2 minutes and serve over equal amounts of cooked noodles in individual bowls.

Top with equal amounts of prawns and serve immediately. Serve the garnish of sliced eschallots, sliced limes, shredded cucumber and Vietnamese mint on a separate plate.

BARRAMUNDI FILLET WITH GREEN CURRY SAUCE & QUICK STIR-FRIED RICE

SERVES 4

→ INGREDIENTS

- 4 x 160 g (6 oz) pieces barramundi fillet (or other firm white fish)
- Spray vegetable oil
- 120 g (4 oz) Thai green curry paste
- 240 ml (8 fl oz) coconut milk
- 300 g (11oz) snake beans, trimmed

QUICK STIR-FRIED RICE

- 2 tablespoons vegetable oil
- 2 eggs, beaten
- 3 rashers bacon, rind removed and diced
- 4 green spring onions, white part minced and the green tops reserved
- 2 cloves garlic, minced
- 650 g (23 oz) long grain rice, cooked
- 3 tablespoons soy sauce

→ METHOD

FOR THE QUICK STIR-FRIED RICE

Heat 1 tablespoon oil in a wok to smoking point. Tip in the eggs and move around very quickly so they set and separate into small pieces. Remove from wok and make sure they are in small pieces. Set to one side. Reheat wok, add the other tablespoon oil and cook the bacon. Stir-fry for 2 minutes or until it starts to crisp. Add the white part of the spring onions with the garlic. Stir and cook for another minute.

Tip in the rice and stir through to reheat. Pour in the soy, add the egg pieces and combine well. Remove from the heat and chop some of the reserved green tops of the spring onion and stir through. Serve immediately.

Mix the curry paste and coconut milk in a saucepan and simmer for 5 minutes, stirring occasionally.

Cut the snake beans into bite-sized pieces and boil until tender. Drain and keep warm.

Spray both sides of the fish with oil and cook on medium-hot plate. The time will depend on the thickness of each piece.

Spoon rice onto a plate and pile snake beans alongside the rice. Place fish on the rice and spoon over the green curry sauce to taste.

MIXED SEAFOOD LINGUINE
SERVES 4

→ INGREDIENTS

- 4 small fish fillets, such as whiting
- 8 medium king prawns, peeled and de-veined, tails left on
- Spray olive oil
- 12 mussels, out of shell
- 8 small sea scallops, cleaned and black membrane removed
- 12 Pacific oysters, out of shell

FOR THE SAUCE

- 2 tablespoons olive oil
- 2 tablespoons butter
- 1 small onion, finely chopped
- 400 g (14 oz) canned crushed tomatoes
- 240 ml (8 fl oz) white wine
- 2 cloves garlic, chopped
- Oregano or marjoram to taste
- Salt and pepper to taste
- 600 g (21 oz) linguine, cooked al dente
- Ciabiatta bread, sliced

→ METHOD

Make sure all the seafood is cleaned and ready to cook. Store covered in the refrigerator.

Make the sauce by heating the oil and butter in a saucepan (I use a wok). When foaming add the onion and cook, stirring, for 2 minutes. Pour in the crushed tomatoes, wine and add the garlic. Simmer for 30 minutes. Remove from heat and keep warm if using shortly; otherwise, cool, cover and refrigerate.

When ready to cook and serve, add the oregano or marjoram and salt and pepper to sauce and take it to the barbecue along with the linguine and raw seafood.

Heat the sauce on the wok ring. Stir and add the mussels and simmer. Cook the fish and prawns by spraying with a little oil and cooking on a medium-hot plate until done.

Meanwhile, add the scallops and oysters to the sauce and stir in. Carefully add the linguine and coat/reheat using tongs to lift and stir.

Take the cooked seafood from the barbecue and keep warm. Serve the pasta and sauce in large individual bowls. Place a cooked fillet on this and top with the prawns. Put the bread into the middle of the table and serve with a green salad.

SPANISH-STYLE SARDINES WITH AIOLI & CHICKPEA CARROT SALAD

Iain Hewitson is a great bloke who adores his food and his influence on the Melbourne restaurant scene and Australian food at large is well recognised. His bar and restaurant, Barney's Bar, on Fitzroy Street in Melbourne's St Kilda is the place to go. He has let me use this recipe from Huey's Best Ever Barbecue Recipes.

→ INGREDIENTS

- 24 whole sardines, cleaned, gutted and butterflied
- Sea salt
- Spray olive oil

HUEY'S AIOLI

- 120 ml (4 fl oz) good mayonnaise
- 3 tablespoons sour cream
- 1 teaspoon Dijon mustard
- 3 cloves garlic, crushed
- 1 tablespoon lemon juice

CARROT AND CHICKPEA SALAD

- 200 g (7 oz) baby carrots, peeled and cut on the diagonal
- 300 g (11 oz) canned chickpeas, drained and rinsed
- 1 teaspoon ground cinnamon
- 1 teaspoon ground cumin
- 1 small red chilli, deseeded and finely sliced
- 1 large lemon, zest and juice
- 2 tablespoons honey
- 120 ml (4 fl oz) olive oil

→ METHOD

Press some sea salt onto the sardines, spray with oil and cook on medium-hot grill until done. I do these in batches of 6–8 as they cook quickly. Cook until done.

Spoon the salad onto the sides of individual dinner plates, pile the sardines beside the salad and spoon a big dollop of aioli beside the sardines and serve immediately.

FOR THE CARROT AND CHICKPEA SALAD

Cook the carrots in boiling water for a few minutes or until just tender. Mix the remaining ingredients, drain the carrots when ready and add to the chickpea mixture. Toss well to combine and leave to cool.

FOR HUEY'S AIOLI

Whisk all the ingredients together for this quick, delicious version of aioli.

DUKKAH-CRUSTED ATLANTIC SALMON WITH TABBOULEH SALAD

SERVES 4

→ INGREDIENTS

- 4 x 150 g (5 oz) Atlantic salmon fillets, skinless and bones removed
- Spray olive oil
- 160 g (5.5 oz) Dukkah, recipe below
- 4 lemon cheeks

TABBOULEH

- 220 g (7.7 oz) spiced bulgur mix (I use Samir's Bulgur Feast mix)
- 240-480 ml (8-16 fl oz) warm water
- 150 g (5 oz) parsley, chopped
- 160 g (5.5 oz) ripe tomatoes, diced
- 1 tablespoon lemon zest, finely shredded
- 3 tablespoons lemon juice
- 2 tablespoons extra virgin olive oil

DUKKAH

- 100 g (4 oz) almonds, skin on
- 60 g (2 oz) pine nuts
- 4 teaspoons linseeds
- 1 teaspoon ground coriander
- 1 teaspoon ground cumin
- 1 teaspoon white sesame seeds
- ½ teaspoon chilli powder
- 1 teaspoon Szechuan peppercorns

→ METHOD

Dry roast the almonds; dry roast pine nuts and linseeds over medium heat. Cool and tip into a food processor. Add the coriander, cumin, sesame seeds, chilli and Szechuan pepper and work to a rough mixture – it should be granular/lumpy and not a paste. Store in an airtight container.

Evenly slice the salmon fillets into pieces around 2–3cm (1in) thick. Spray flesh side lightly with oil and press into Dukkah on flat dinner plate. Lift and shake off excess. Spray medium-hot flat plate with oil and cook the fillets Dukkah-side down first. After a minute, spray the other side of the fish pieces and, with a long spatula gently flip the fish over. The cooking time will depend on the thickness of the pieces.

Put the salad onto individual plates, top with fish and serve with lemon cheeks to one side.

FOR THE TABBOULEH

Make the salad first by soaking the bulgur mix in the water for 30 minutes. After that, add the other ingredients and mix thoroughly. I like to leave this mixture sit for at least 3 hours before use.

SNAPPER FILLETS WITH CHIVE VERJUICE BUTTER & SALMON ROE

`SERVES 4`

→ INGREDIENTS

- 4 x 150 g (5 oz) snapper fillets
- Spray olive oil
- 24 large snow peas, topped and tailed
- 4 tablespoons salmon roe

CHIVE VERJUICE BUTTER

- 150 g (5 oz) butter, at room temperature
- 15 g (0.5 oz) chives, chopped
- 1 tablespoon verjuice
- 1 teaspoon ground white pepper

→ METHOD

FOR THE CHIVE VERJUICE BUTTER

Put the butter, chives, verjuice and pepper into a food processor and pulse until combined. Lift out with a spatula onto a piece of clingwrap or waxed paper. Shape into a log/roll and freeze to set for at least 30 minutes or longer so the flavours meld.

Trim the fish fillet and check for scales. Pat dry with towelling and spray with oil. Cook on medium-hot plate, starting with flesh side down. Spray the skin side of the fillet and turn after a couple of minutes. The thickness of the fish will determine how long they cook on this side. When you turn each fillet, put the spatula/flipper on top to stop the fillet curling.

Boil (or microwave) the snow peas until done.

Serve the fish on individual plates with the snow peas alongside and top with a good thick slice of the chive butter and with a tablespoon of roe on top of the butter.

RAINBOW TROUT WITH PANFRIED RED CABBAGE & SALMON ROE CREAM

SERVES 4

→ INGREDIENTS

- 8 medium Rainbow Trout fillets
- Spray olive oil
- 350 g (12 oz) red cabbage, finely shredded
- ½ green apple, cored and chopped finely
- 2 tablespoons vegetable oil
- Sea salt and ground white pepper to taste

- 2 tablespoons red wine vinegar
- 300 g (10 oz) green peas, cooked and kept hot
- 240 ml (8 fl oz) sour cream, at room temperature
- 1 tablespoon dill, chopped
- 50 g (1.5 oz) salmon roe

→ METHOD

Trim the trout fillets if necessary and remove as many bones as possible. Refrigerate until ready to cook.

Tip the cabbage, apple and oil into a large bowl and toss to coat. Sprinkle with salt and pepper to taste. Cook on a medium-hot plate by lifting and tossing to keep the cabbage moving. Heap, pour on the vinegar and cover with hood or large stainless steel bowl and steam/cook for a minute.

Lift from barbecue and keep warm. Alternatively, this can be done in a wok on the ring.

Cook the fish by spraying with fillets with oil and putting them onto a medium-hot plate, skin-side down. Cook for 1–2 minutes and turn. These fillets are generally quite thin and cook quickly so judge the cooking time by the thickness of the fillets.

Mix the sour cream, dill and roe together very carefully so as not to break the roe.

Serve by putting the cabbage into the middle of individual dinner plates, lean the fish against the cabbage, spoon the peas around and serve the cream on the side for everyone to take as much as they want.

PROSCIUTTO PRAWNS WITH ROCKET AIOLI
SERVES 4

Garlic varies in its intensity and you need to be aware of this. In testing this recipe twice with garlic from two different sources, I got two very different results. Go for large garlic cloves if they are not so powerful. How do you find out about the intensity? Cut a small piece off the end of the garlic you are using and eat. If it is strong, cut back on the amount used or blanch the garlic in boiling water for 30 seconds.

→ INGREDIENTS

- 24 large green king prawns, with middle section peeled and de-veined
- 24 bamboo skewers, soaked in water for 30 minutes or metal skewers
- 12–24 slices prosciutto (this depends on how long each slice is. If really long, cut across to give two equal pieces. Larger prawns will require the whole piece)

ROCKET AIOLI

- 4 medium cloves garlic
- ½ teaspoon sea salt
- 2 egg yolks
- ½ teaspoon lemon juice
- 25 g (0.9 oz) blanched and well drained rocket
- 125 ml (4 oz) olive oil

→ METHOD

Take each prawn and thread it onto a skewer starting from the tail. Roll each prawn in prosciutto so as to cover all the prawn. Store on clingwrap-covered plate in the refrigerator until ready to use.

Cook the prawns on a medium-hot flat plate, turning regularly for even cooking. When the top (head end) of the prawns are completely white, they are ready to eat. The prosciutto wraps around the prawn very tightly as it cooks.

Serve with the aioli to one side and with lemon and olive oil-dressed rocket leaves.

FOR THE ROCKET AIOLI

Put the garlic, salt, egg yolks, lemon juice and rocket into the food processor bowl and work for 30 seconds. When this mixture is starting to thicken, slowly pour the oil down the feeder shoot. As it takes, you can add the oil a little more quickly until finished.

OCEAN TROUT ON NICOISE SALAD
SERVES 4

→ INGREDIENTS

- 4 x 150 g (5 oz) ocean trout fillets
- Spray olive oil
- 150 g (5 oz) Desiree potato slices, 2 cm (1 in) thick and boiled until cooked but firm
- 3 Roma tomatoes, trimmed and cut into wedges
- 200 g (7 oz) green beans, whole, trimmed and blanched
- 2 hard-boiled eggs, peeled and quartered lengthwise
- 3 tablespoons extra virgin olive oil
- 2 tablespoons white wine vinegar
- 8 anchovy fillets
- 20 kalamata olives
- Cracked black pepper to taste

→ METHOD

Spray the fillets with a little oil and cook on hot plate of barbecue for 2 minutes; turn and cook a further 2 minutes. This fish is best cooked medium so the time cooking will depend on the thickness of your fish. Lift and let cool to room temperature.

Heap potatoes, tomatoes, beans and hard-boiled egg quarters into the centre of a large plate or platter. Scatter the olives around the vegetables and eggs.

Mix the olive oil and vinegar together and spoon over the ingredients on the plate.

Top with ocean trout, sprinkle with black pepper and serve.

LOBSTER MEDALLIONS WITH THAI CUCUMBER & ASIAN LEAVES

SERVES 4

→ INGREDIENTS

- 12 medium lobster medallions
- 60 ml (2 fl oz) vegetable oil
- ¼ teaspoon sea salt
- Ground black pepper to taste
- 100 g (4 oz) mixed Asian leaves

THAI-FLAVOURED CUCUMBERS

- 4 tablespoons coconut/rice vinegar
- 3 tablespoon white sugar
- 1 small red chilli, deseeded and minced

- 1 large Lebanese cucumber, seeds removed and finely diced
- 1 red eschallot, finely diced
- 1 tablespoon green ginger root, minced
- 1 clove garlic, crushed
- 1 tablespoon coriander leaves, chopped
- 1 tablespoon vegetable oil
- 1 tablespoon fish sauce

→ METHOD

FOR THE THAI-FLAVOURED CUCUMBERS

Mix the vinegar and sugar together and stir to dissolve. Add all the other ingredients, toss and marinate for 1 hour before serving.

Pat the lobster dry and brush both sides with oil. Cook on medium-hot plate and sprinkle with salt and pepper as you cook. Turn when done and sprinkle with salt and pepper. Turn only once as they cook through quite quickly. Lift from the barbecue and keep warm.

Distribute the leaves into the centre of individual dinner plates. Drain the cucumbers and toss over the leaves. Serve the lobster beside medallions sitting beside the salad.

BABY SNAPPER WITH CHEESY CREAMY POTATOES AND MINTED PEAS

SERVES 4

→ INGREDIENTS

- 4 plate-sized baby snappers
- 1 small lemon, cut into quarters
- 12 garlic chives
- 80 g (2.8 oz) butter, melted
- 1 teaspoon sea salt
- 1 teaspoon cracked black pepper
- 4 large sheets of aluminium foil, sprayed with oil
- 200 g (7 oz) peas, frozen or fresh
- 1 tablespoon butter
- 3 tablespoons mint, finely chopped
- Cheesy creamy potatoes (see page 49)

→ METHOD

Wash the fish cavity with cold water and dry with absorbent paper. Cut 2 deep slashes into each side of each fish. Place the fish on individual pieces of oiled foil – stuff the cavity with the lemon quarter and 3 garlic chives, cut to fit the cavity.

Spoon over the melted butter and sprinkle with salt and pepper. Repeat for each fish. Wrap the fish in the foil and refrigerate for 30 minutes. Ensure that the foil is tight around the fish so the juices cannot escape in the cooking process.

Bring the fish to room temperature for 15 minutes before placing them on a medium–hot flat plate and cooking for 6–7 minutes each side.

Remove from plate and serve on individual dinner plates. Cover the peas with water and boil for 2–3 minutes, strain and return to saucepan with butter and mint. Put on lid and toss to coat the peas with butter and mint. Turn out into serving bowl. Put the cheesy creamy potatoes and peas into the middle of the table.

FENNEL & PEPPER CRUSTED BLUE EYE WITH GOAT'S CHEESE SALAD

SERVES 4

→ INGREDIENTS

- 4 x 150 g (5 oz) blue-eye cod steaks
- 1 tablespoon fennel seeds
- ½ tablespoon white peppercorns
- ¼ teaspoon sea salt
- Spray olive oil

GOAT'S CHEESE SALAD

- 150 g (5.3 oz) mixed salad leaves

- 100 g (3.5 oz) semi-roasted tomatoes, chopped
- 100 g (3.5 oz) dry goat's cheese, crumbled or cut into dice
- 3 tablespoons extra virgin olive oil
- 1 tablespoon balsamic vinegar

→ METHOD

Pat the fish dry. Roughly crush the fennel seeds, peppercorns and salt in a mortar and pestle. Sprinkle equal amounts onto each side of the fish and pat into each fillet.

Heat half the flat plate to high, spray fish with oil and cook on a medium plate – spray with oil and turn after a minute and cook through. The time will depend on the thickness of the fish which will be firm to touch but not breaking up when it is done.

Meanwhile, have the leaves, tomatoes and cheese in a bowl; toss with the oil and balsamic vinegar.

Serve the fish on individual plates with the salad into the middle of the table.

CUTTLEFISH WITH CHORIZO, CAPSICUM & PINE NUT SALAD
SERVES 4

→ INGREDIENTS

- 400 g (14 oz) cuttlefish, body only
- 60 ml (2 fl oz) good olive oil
- 250 g (9 oz) chorizo (Spanish sausage), cut into 1 cm (½ in) thick slices
- 150 g (5 oz) yellow capsicum (pepper), deseeded and cut into bite size pieces
- 60 g (2 oz) pine nuts, toasted
- 20 grape tomatoes, halved
- 2 tablespoons zest of lemon, finely grated
- 60 ml (2 fl oz) lemon juice
- 2 tablespoons Italian parsley, roughly chopped
- Sea salt to taste
- 2 tablespoons good olive oil
- 100 g (4 oz) mixed salad leaves

→ METHOD

Cut the cuttlefish open to form one large flat piece. Trim and with a very sharp knife score the flesh into diamond shapes. Cut into bite-sized pieces and put into a bowl.

Pour the first lot of olive oil in and toss the cuttlefish in it. Let sit for 15 minutes and if any longer, refrigerate.

Put the capsicum, pine nuts and tomato halves into the salad bowl; mix the lemon zest, juice and salt and pour over the capsicum mix. Add the chopped parsley and toss together – refrigerate until ready for use.

Put the cuttlefish onto medium-hot flat plate, scored side down. These pieces will curl so you need to move them around to ensure all the surfaces are exposed to the heat. Cuttlefish cooks quickly so do not overcook as it toughens. Lift from the barbecue and put into a bowl. Tip over the capsicum mixture and toss to coat and cool the fish. Let rest.

Put the chorizo slices on the hot grill; let crisp and brown and remove when done.

Pour the second lot of olive oil over the salad leaves and toss. Divide the sausage slices into equal amounts on individual plates. Add some salad onto the top of the sausage slices and put pieces of the cuttlefish and capsicum mixture on top and around the salad. Spoon any juices from the cuttlefish over if you like.

PRAWN KEBABS WITH PINEAPPLE CORIANDER SALSA

SERVES 4

→ INGREDIENTS

- 16 green king prawns, peeled completely and de-veined
- 3 tablespoons pineapple juice
- 1 tablespoon vegetable oil
- 1 teaspoon Thai green curry paste
- 4 stainless steel skewers or bamboo skewers soaked in water for 30 minutes
- Spray vegetable oil

PINEAPPLE CORIANDER SALSA

- 60 g (2 oz) white onion, roughly chopped
- 150 g (5 oz) pineapple, peeled and roughly chopped
- 1 small red chilli, flesh only and chopped
- 50 g (1.8 oz) coriander leaves

→ METHOD

Toss the prawns with the juice, oil and curry paste. Let sit for 15 minutes. Thread the prawns onto the skewers so you have four on each one. This is best done by curling the prawns in their natural form and then pushing the skewer through so as to get four horseshoe shapes in a row.

Spray with oil and cook on medium-hot plate for 1 minute; spray with oil and turn again and cook through. Baste with the pineapple marinade at least once.

Serve on large platter with pineapple salsa spooned over.

FOR THE PINEAPPLE CORIANDER SALSA

Put all ingredients into a food processor and pulse to a rough paste. This salsa is quite runny and is best served immediately.

CALAMARI WITH LIME JUICE AND CORIANDER
SERVES 4

→ INGREDIENTS

- 6 medium calamari tubes, cleaned
- 3 fresh tablespoons lime juice
- 1 tablespoon peanut oil
- 1 small red chilli, deseeded and minced
- 1 root coriander, washed and minced

- 3 teaspoons fish sauce (nam pla)
- 1 teaspoon palm sugar
- Spray oil
- Sprigs of coriander, washed and crisped in refrigerator

→ METHOD

Slit the tubes down one side and open to lay flat, skin side down, and score finely. Cut into bite-sized pieces.

Make a marinade by combining the lime juice, peanut oil, chilli, coriander root, fish sauce and sugar. Mix well. Soak the scored calamari in this marinade for 15 minutes.

Lift the calamari from the marinade and drain off any excess juices.

Spray a hot plate with oil and put the calamari onto it. Cook in small batches.

Tumble and turn the pieces, cooking for no longer than 2 minutes.

Decorate with scattered torn coriander leaves and serve.

ALMOND PARSLEY-CRUSTED SNAPPER FILLETS
SERVES 4

For this fish dish I suggest you use the thinner tail end of the snapper fillets.

INGREDIENTS

- 4 x 180 g (6 oz) snapper fillets
- 15 g (0.5 oz) flat leaf parsley, finely chopped
- 15 g (0.5 oz) green spring onions, finely chopped
- 40 g (1.4 oz) almonds, skin on, chopped
- 1 clove garlic, minced
- 1 tablespoon capers, rinsed
- 30 g (1 oz) breadcrumbs, fresh
- 1 egg white
- Spray vegetable oil
- 4 lemon wedges

METHOD

Trim the fish fillets if necessary and refrigerate until ready to cook.

Mix the parsley, spring onions, almonds, garlic, capers and breadcrumbs. Whisk the egg white with a fork and tip half into the crust mixture and tumble to combine well.

Pat the fish dry with paper towel and brush with remaining half egg white. Spoon and pat a layer of the parsley mix onto each fish fillet. Spray a flat baking tray with oil, line with baking paper and spray the paper with oil. Carefully lift the snapper fillets onto the baking tray.

Put a cake cooling rack or similar onto the hot flat plate and sit the fish on that. Cook in moderately hot barbecue with the hood down for 6–8 minutes. Time depends on the thickness of the fish fillet.

Lift and serve with lemon wedge to one side and a potato salad or green salad.

CHARGRILLED BABY OCTOPUS WITH MANGO SALSA

SERVES 4

→ INGREDIENTS

- 20 baby octopus, cleaned and tenderised
- 2 tablespoons vegetable oil
- ¼ teaspoon sea salt
- 500 g (16 oz) mango flesh, diced into 1 cm (0.4 in) cubes
- 100 g (4 oz) red onion, finely diced
- 1 large green fruity chilli, deseeded and finely chopped
- 2 tablespoons orange juice
- 1 tablespoon orange zest, finely grated

→ METHOD

Put the octopus in with the oil and salt and toss; let sit for 10 minutes. This eliminates the need to oil the barbecue plate when cooking.

Mix the mango, onion, chilli, juice and zest; sit for 10 minutes.

Cook the octopus on a very hot plate and toss to cook evenly. Do not overcook as they go tough – once firm they are ready to go. Put the salsa into the middle of a large plate and place the octopus around the salsa. Serve with a good green salad to turn it into a more substantial starter.

CRAB OMELETTES WITH SPICY CUCUMBER SALSA
SERVES 4

→ INGREDIENTS

- 8 medium eggs, free range if possible
- Salt to taste
- Ground black pepper, to taste
- 240 g (9 oz) crab meat, chopped
- Spray oil
- 4 teaspoons butter

SPICY CUCUMBER SALSA

- 4 tablespoons coconut/rice vinegar
- 3 tablespoons white sugar
- 1 small red chilli, deseeded and minced
- 1 Lebanese cucumber, seeds removed and finely diced
- 1 red shallot, finely diced
- 1 tablespoon ginger, grated
- 1 clove garlic, crushed
- 1 tablespoon coriander leaves, chopped
- 1 tablespoon vegetable oil
- 1 tablespoon fish sauce

→ METHOD

Beat the eggs well with salt to taste, in four separate containers. I use teacups.

Divide the crab into four even batches.

Spray a low-heat, very clean barbecue plate with oil in a circle about 22 cm (9 in) in diameter.

Add a teaspoon of butter and, as it melts, spread around that circle with a spatula. Tip on the first two beaten eggs and very quickly pull/push the eggs into a circular shape and let the eggs start to set. Cut holes into the setting egg mixture to let the uncooked egg move through and set.

When firm, which will take about a minute, spoon the crab mixture down the centre and fold each side over the crab meat. Flip the omelette over and let sit for 30 seconds or until set.

Lift from the barbecue, keep warm and repeat with the other three batches.

When all have been cooked, serve at room temperature onto individual plates. Spoon a little drained cucumber salsa on the side of each omelette.

FOR THE SPICY CUCUMBER SALSA

Mix the vinegar and sugar together and stir to dissolve. Add all the ingredients and marinate for 1 hour before serving.

MEXICAN SPICED OCEAN TROUT FAJITAS

SERVES 4

→ INGREDIENTS

- 500 g (18 oz) ocean trout fillets, skin and pin bones removed
- 2 tablespoons of corn oil (or light olive oil)
- 2 tablespoons white vinegar
- 1 teaspoon Mexican chilli powder
- 1 teaspoon allspice, ground

- ½ teaspoon oregano, ground
- Olive oil spray
- 8 wheat flour tortillas
- 100 g (3.5 oz) shredded lettuce
- 1 small Spanish onion, finely sliced
- 50 g (1.8 oz) carrot, grated
- red Tabasco sauce (optional)

→ METHOD

Cut the fish into 2 cm (0.8 in) wide x 8 cm (3 in) long strips; mix the oil, vinegar, chilli powder, allspice and oregano in a bowl and add the fish strips. Cover and refrigerate for 20 minutes.

Spray a medium–hot flat plate with oil, and add the strips. Spread them evenly and do only as many as you can control. As ocean trout does not like to be overcooked, I normally cook 10 strips at a time and turn them only once. Remove from heat and keep warm.

Spray the tortillas with oil and heat very quickly, 30 seconds each side, on the hot open grill. Remove and stack on plate.

Assemble fajitas by putting fish strips near the middle of each tortilla, top with lettuce, onion and grated carrot.

Roll and eat immediately. You can drizzle on some Tabasco sauce if you like.

ALMOND, LEMON AND PERI-PERI GRILLED FILLETS OF FISH

`SERVES 4`

→ INGREDIENTS

- 4 x 150 g (5.3 oz) fillets white fish (I use Dory fillets)
- 60 g (2 oz) almonds, chopped with the skin on
- 5 tablespoons fat-free mayonnaise
- 2 tablespoons lemon juice
- 1 teaspoon medium Peri-Peri (chilli sauce)
- 1 teaspoon cumin powder
- 100 g (3.5 oz) mixed lettuce leaves
- Shredded zest and juice of one lemon

→ METHOD

Trim fillets if needed.

Mix the almonds, mayonnaise, lemon juice, Peri-Peri and cumin together. Smear the fish fillets with this mixture and let sit for 20 minutes on a baking tray.

Heat the grill to very hot and cook the fish under the grill for 5–10 minutes.

Dress the salad leaves with the zest and lemon juice. Use as much of the lemon juice as you like – or as little.

Serve the cooked fish with the salad and a carbohydrate, such as hot couscous.

PRAWN GLASS NOODLE SALAD
SERVES 4

→ INGREDIENTS

- 300 g (10.5 oz) medium cooked king prawns, peeled and deveined
- 125 g (4.5 oz) dried bean thread noodles
- 75 g (2.5 oz) carrot, peeled and cut into strips
- 75 g (2.5 oz) Lebanese cucumber, shredded, seeds removed
- 1 small red onion, finely sliced
- 60 g (2 oz) snow pea sprouts
- 60 g (2 oz) red capsicum (pepper), finely sliced
- coriander leaves to garnish

FOR THE DRESSING
- 1 tablespoon natural pineapple juice
- 1 tablespoon lime zest, finely grated
- 3 tablespoons lime juice
- 1 tablespoon raw sugar
- 60 ml (2 fl oz) lite coconut milk
- 1 tablespoon fish sauce (nam pla)

→ METHOD

Chop the prawns into halves or smaller pieces if you like.

Put the noodles into a large bowl and pour boiling water over to cover them. Let sit for 5–7 minutes then strain and run under cold water to stop cooking. Tip the noodles into a mixing bowl and allow to cool. Add all the other ingredients, except for the coriander leaves, and toss gently using your hands.

Make the dressing by combining all the ingredients. Stir well to ensure the sugar is dissolved. Pour the dressing over the noodle ingredients and toss gently. Top with the coriander leaves and serve.

These noodles are sometimes called mung bean noodles. You can replace them with rice vermicelli noodles if you like.

TUNA-STUFFED TOMATOES WITH ROCKET SALAD

SERVES 4

→ INGREDIENTS

- 4 ripe firm tomatoes, around 100 g (3.5 oz) each
- 4 tablespoons canned/bottled corn kernels
- 3 tablespoons red onion, diced
- 185 g (6.5 oz) tuna in spring water
- 2 tablespoons parsley, chopped
- 1 tablespoon coarsely ground black pepper
- 2 tablespoons lemon juice

- 8 cooked and skinned baby beetroots, quartered

FOR THE SALAD

- 2 tablespoons linseed oil
- 1 teaspoon seeded mustard
- 3 tablespoons lemon juice
- 1 tablespoon tomato flesh, diced
- 50 g (1.8 oz) rocket leaves
- 30 g (1 oz) mixed leaves

→ METHOD

Cut the tops from the tomatoes and keep. Ease the flesh out of the tomatoes with a teaspoon and roughly chop. Cut the flesh from the tops, roughly chop and add.

Mix the corn, onion, tuna, parsley, pepper, lemon juice and tomato flesh. Spoon the mixture into each tomato and press it in with the back of the spoon. Cover with cling wrap and store in refrigerator until ready to serve.

Whisk the oil and mustard, add lemon juice and 1 tablespoon tomato flesh.

Add the rocket and mixed leaves to the dressing and toss to coat. Put an equal amount into the centre of four plates and add beetroot pieces around the edge of the salad leaves. Sit a tomato in the middle of the leaves, put the top on each one and serve.

Any leftover filling makes an excellent sandwich the next day. The tuna mixture develops such beautiful flavour that I make the mixture the day before stuffing the tomatoes.

OYSTERS, SALMON ROE AND LIME DRESSING
SERVES 4

Can I live without oysters? No way! I have adored them for years. When I had my first restaurant I used to sail regularly and we would pick small oysters from the rocks.

→ INGREDIENTS

- 24 medium to large oysters, on the shell
- 15 g (0.5 oz) salmon roe
- 60 ml (2 fl oz) lime juice
- 1 teaspoon Sichuan peppercorns, crushed
- 1 teaspoon salt-reduced Tamari soy sauce

→ METHOD

Make sure the oysters are clean; sit them on individual, flat plates (see note).

Spoon an equal amount of roe onto each oyster.

Mix the juice, peppercorns and soy sauce well. When ready to serve, spoon a little of the dressing around the roe and over the oyster.

You can see that these have a good sodium content, so as you would serve them as an starter course, ensure the main course you serve with them has a low sodium content.

Sometimes I shred outside lettuce leaves to make sure the oysters sit upright.

WHITING FILLETS WITH SWEET POTATO AND TURNIP CAKE

`SERVES 4`

→ INGREDIENTS

- 600 g (21 oz) whiting fillets
- 1 egg white, lightly whipped
- 90 g (3 oz) rye flour
- Spray olive oil
- Rocket leaves to taste
- 200 g (7 oz) green beans, topped and tailed
- 4 lemon wedges

FOR THE CAKE

- ½ medium-sized onion, finely diced
- 250 g (8.8 oz) swede (turnip), peeled, grated
- 200 g (7 oz) white sweet potato, peeled, grated
- ½ teaspoon allspice
- ½ teaspoon dried chilli flakes
- 1 large free-range egg
- 2 tablespoons wholemeal self-raising flour

→ METHOD

Trim the fillets if necessary and refrigerate until ready to use. Preheat oven to 180ºC.

Make the cake by mixing and combining all remaining ingredients well. Line a 20cm (8in) square by 5cm (2in) deep baking dish with baking paper. Spray with a film of oil and spoon in the mixture. Pat down with your wet hands, spray with a film of oil and bake for 60 minutes.

Pat the fish dry, dip in egg white then into the rye flour – shake off all excess flour and put onto a lightly oiled tray, lined with baking paper. Spray with some oil and bake until browned and crisped – around 15 minutes.

Let the cake rest for 10 minutes before inverting the baking dish onto a cutting board. Cut into four equal-sized squares, then into triangles to serve under the fish fillets. Serve triangles and fish on a bed of rocket leaves or put the rocket to one side with lightly-steamed green beans and serve with a lemon wedge.

This cake is a beauty that is excellent served cold or at room temperature. I like it under canned salmon for lunch with a side salad.

MANDARIN VODKA CHERVIL OYSTERS
SERVES 4

→ INGREDIENTS

- 24 Pacific oysters, freshly shucked
- 30–40 ml (1-1.3 fl oz) mandarin vodka
- 6–8 mandarin segments, drained from can and cut into small pieces
- chervil sprigs
- rock salt, for serving

→ METHOD

Ensure the oysters are clear of visible shell grit. Take them to the barbecue with the vodka. Put them on a hot open grill and spoon some vodka over the oysters – do not overfill them because the vodka will ignite if it spills over the edge. Do only 6–8 oysters at a time.

They are ready to go when there is a little bubbling around the edge of the oyster flesh – do NOT overcook!

Remove from the barbecue, top with a piece of mandarin segment and some chervil sprigs – serve on a cocktail napkin, around the barbecue, while warm.

SCALLOP AND BACON KEBABS
SERVES 4

→ INGREDIENTS
- 16 scallops, roe removed
- 16 parsley, leaves only
- 16 x 10 cm (4 in)-long pieces bacon, rind removed
- 16 stainless steel skewers or bamboo skewers, soaked in water for 30 minutes
- 4 lemon cheeks

→ METHOD
Remove the little black membrane from the side of each scallop.

Sit each scallop on the end of a piece of bacon – top with a parsley leaf and roll the bacon around each scallop. Thread 4 wrapped scallops onto each skewer.

Cook on medium–hot flat plate for 2 minutes each side and serve with the lemon cheeks.

As scallops are so delicate it is always good to offer them the protection of a wrap such as bacon. Oh! and there's the flavour combo... yum!

BLACK MUSSELS WITH GARLIC AND RED WINE BUTTER
SERVES 4

→ INGREDIENTS

- 24 black mussels, cleaned and beards removed
- 320 g (8.2 oz) garlic and red wine butter
- fresh bread, a baguette or ciabiatta

GARLIC AND RED WINE BUTTER
- 250 g (8.8 oz) salted butter
- 4 cloves garlic, chopped
- 2 tablespoons parsley, chopped
- 3 tablespoons red wine
- ½ tablespoon black pepper

→ METHOD

To make the butter combine all the ingredients in a processor or by whipping with a fork or whisk.

Put the mussels onto a medium-hot open grill plate. Very shortly they will start to open – lift each one into a bowl as they do. When all are removed and cool enough to handle, discard the empty top shell from each mussel. Dot each mussel with some butter (don't overload as the butter will melt and spill onto the flames). Put back onto the open grill and lower the hood for 1 minute – mussels are cooked when bubbling and the butter has melted.

Serve on individual plates with melted garlic and red wine butter if you like and plenty of good bread for dunking into the juices.

Black mussels must be fresh. You can tell by tipping them into a sinkful of water – discard any floaters. They can take a long time to clean – scrubbing and removing the beard, which it anchors itself within the sea.

BOSTON BAY CLAMS IN BASIL AND WHITE WINE
SERVES 4

→ INGREDIENTS

- 48 Boston Bay (or other) clams
- 2 spring onions, roughly chopped
- 2 cloves garlic, roughly chopped
- 2 bay leaves
- 12 peppercorns
- 240 ml (8 fl oz) dry white wine
- 480 ml (16 fl oz) fish stock
- 2 tablespoons Italian basil, chopped
- 3 tablespoons salted butter, very cold, diced into 3cm (1.2 in) cubes
- 4–8 slices garlic bread

→ METHOD

Make sure the clams are cleaned and ready for cooking. Put the onions, garlic, bay leaves and peppercorns into a stainless steel frying pan or similar. I have one that goes into the oven and the barbecue. If you have a domed lid for it, all the better.

Add the clams, wine and fish stock. If you have a lid, fit it on now and put onto a very hot open grill – if no lid, drop the hood and cook. If no hood or lid, cover with stainless steel bowl or similar. Bring to the boil and then simmer for 5 minutes.

Remove from the barbecue and distribute the clams into large individual bowls. Return pan to heat. Add the basil and cook for 30 seconds. Remove from the heat and swirl in the butter. Pour equal amounts over the clams and serve with garlic bread.

These clams grow in the pristine waters of Boston Bay in South Australia – they are all ready to go when you buy them.

VEGETARIAN

GRILLED PIDE &
BEETROOT HUMMUS
SERVES 4

→ INGREDIENTS

- 12 fingers pide bread, roughly 4 cm (1.5 in) wide
- Spray oil

FOR THE BEETROOT HUMMUS

- 325 g (11.5 oz) cooked pinto beans
- 200g (7oz) cooked beetroot, chopped
- 2 tablespoons lime juice
- 2 tablespoon organic tahini
- 1 teaspoon white sesame seeds
- ½ teaspoon ground white pepper
- 1 teaspoon powdered cumin
- 120 ml (4 fl oz) olive oil

→ METHOD

FOR THE BEETROOT HUMMUS

Puree all ingredients to a rough paste in a processor or with a hand blender. Store in airtight container in the refrigerator for up to 7 days.

Spray pide fingers with oil and crisp/brown on the hot grill. Serve the hummus in a bowl surrounded by the warm pide fingers.

CRISPY FOCACCIA WITH SPICY BLACK EYE BEAN SPREAD & ROCKET

SERVES 4

→ INGREDIENTS

- 2 x 12 cm (5 in) square pieces focaccia
- Garlic spray oil
- Spicy Eye Bean spread (see recipe below)
- 1 medium Lebanese cucumber, finely sliced into rounds
- 80 g (2.8 oz) sundried tomatoes, roughly chopped
- 100 g (3.5 oz) rocket leaves, crisped
- 90 g (3.2 oz) Romano cheese, grated
- Extra virgin olive oil
- Ground black pepper

SPICY BLACK EYE BEAN PASTE

- 250 g (9 oz) dried black-eye beans, soaked
- 4 cloves garlic, poached
- 2 tablespoons lime juice
- 1 teaspoon powdered cumin
- 1 teaspoon powdered nutmeg
- ½ teaspoon ground white pepper
- ¼ teaspoon powdered chilli
- ½ teaspoon salt
- 2 tablespoons virgin olive oil
- 1 tablespoon parsley, chopped

→ METHOD

Cut the focaccia through the middle to give four even squares/rectangles. Spray the cut side with garlic oil. Brown and crisp both sides on a medium-hot grill.

Spread the black eye bean paste thickly onto the cut side of focaccia. Evenly distribute cucumber slices and tomatoes and top with rocket leaves on top of the spread – don't worry if some of them slip off – and add the cheese. Drizzle over a little oil and sprinkle the pepper. Serve immediately.

FOR THE SPICY BLACK EYE BEAN PASTE

Cook the beans at a simmer until starting to break down. Strain and reserve a cup of the cooking liquid.

Put all the ingredients except for the oil and parsley into a food processor and work into a paste. You may need to add some cooking liquid to make the paste the consistency you like but it should be smooth and creamy.

Tip from the processor bowl and smooth over the top. Spoon over the olive oil and sprinkle with the parsley. Serve as it is or keep refrigerated for up to five days.

PUMPKIN & PARMESAN SOUFFLE
SERVES 4

→ INGREDIENTS

- 30 g (1 oz) butter, melted
- 2 tablespoons dry breadcrumbs, finely grated
- 60 g (2 oz) salted butter
- 60 g (2 oz) plain flour
- 500 ml (17 fl oz) milk, heated not boiled
- 3 large eggs, separated
- 300 g (11 oz) steamed pumpkin, finely mashed and cooled
- 2 tablespoons parmesan cheese, grated
- 1 teaspoon nutmeg, finely grated
- Salt and white pepper to taste
- 4 teaspoons sour cream (optional)

→ METHOD

Preheat barbecue to 180°C.

Brush 4–5 soufflé dishes with the melted butter. Line the inside with breadcrumbs. Make sure you shake out any excess crumbs and refrigerate the soufflé bowls. Remove 10 minutes before use.

Melt the salted butter in a saucepan. Stir in the flour and stir over medium heat until the mixture is going sandy in colour. Stir or whisk in the milk over medium heat in three batches. Stir or whisk quickly to ensure no lumps. Stir for 3 minutes once all the milk is incorporated. Remove from heat and let cool for 5 minutes before the next step.

Fold in the egg yolks, pumpkin, cheese, nutmeg and salt and pepper. Whisk the egg whites until they are light and fluffy. Not firm peaks, just soft.

Spoon 1 large tablespoon of the egg whites into the warm pumpkin mixture. Fold in the rest of the whites. Do this gently so as not to lose the trapped air in the egg whites. Spoon equal amounts into the individual soufflé dishes and cook for 18–20 minutes or until firm to touch and browned on top.

Serve immediately with a dressed green salad. If you use the sour cream, break open the top with a spoon and drop the sour cream inside.

THAI-INSPIRED PUMPKIN SOUP
SERVES 4

→ INGREDIENTS

- 1 small onion, diced
- 2 tablespoons celery, diced
- 2 tablespoons tomatoes, chopped
- 2–3 tablespoons Thai red curry paste
- 500 g (18 oz) blue pumpkin, peeled and roughly diced
- 1 tablespoon coriander seeds, pounded in the mortar and pestle, or ground coriander
- 240 ml (8 fl oz) fat-free evaporated milk

→ METHOD

Pour 120 ml (4 fl oz) of water into a suitable saucepan and bring to the boil; add the onion, celery and tomato and cook for 1 minute. Stir in the red curry paste and add the pumpkin. Coat well then add 1 litre (34 fl oz) of water.

Simmer for 30 minutes or until the pumpkin is breaking down.

Puree and return to saucepan with the coriander. Stir in the evaporated milk while reheating – do not boil. Serve in equal quantities.

Serve with two slices of bread – if offering as light lunch – or one slice of bread if using this scrummy soup for a starter.

VEGETARIAN BURGER, RATATOUILLE AND GREEN PEAS

→ INGREDIENTS

- 4 vegetarian burgers/patties
- Spray olive oil
- 200 g (7 oz) green peas (frozen)

FOR THE RATATOUILLE

- 240 ml (8 fl oz) salt-reduced vegetable stock
- 1 large onion, peeled and diced roughly
- 1 medium eggplant (aubergine), evenly diced (2cm (0.8in) cubes)
- 2 medium zucchini (courgette), evenly diced (2cm (0.8in) cubes)
- 325 g (11.5 oz) tomatoes, diced
- 2 cloves garlic, crushed
- 2 bay leaves
- 3 pieces fresh orange skin, no pith

→ METHOD

Make the ratatouille by combining all ingredients in a large saucepan and cooking at a simmer for at least 60 minutes. Stir regularly and make the day before use for the best results.

Spray the burgers with a film of oil and cook under the griller or in a non-stick frying pan. Cook/heat the peas in the microwave or by boiling.

Put the cooked burger on the plate and spoon ratatouille onto part of the burger. Spoon equal amount of peas onto the plate. Serve with two slices of good bread.

Any leftover ratatouille is brilliant as a sandwich-filler or just to snack on. I first saw my friend, Lyndey Milan, use orange peel in this delightful dish from the south of France—what a difference it makes!

RICE NOODLES & BOK CHOY SALAD WITH GINGER CHILLI SOY DRESSING

SERVES 4

→ INGREDIENTS

- 8 baby bok choy, halved, washed and well drained
- Spray vegetable oil
- 250 g (9 oz) rice vermicelli noodles, rehydrated
- 60 g (2 oz) green spring onions, roughly chopped
- 120 g (4 oz) carrots, peeled and shredded
- 120 g (4 oz) yellow capsicum (pepper), deseeded and in fine strips
- 2 tablespoons sesame seeds, toasted

FOR THE DRESSING
- 2 tablespoons green ginger root, minced
- 2 tablespoons red chilli, minced and with seeds left in
- 1 clove garlic, minced
- 240 ml (8 fl oz) soy sauce
- 1 tablespoon honey
- ½ teaspoon sesame oil

→ METHOD

Make sure the bok choy has been washed thoroughly and drained well. Spray cut side with oil and quickly cook (mark) on very hot grill. I do this by putting the stalk part onto the grill but let the leaves hang over the edge—in that way, the softer green leaves do not get dried out and burnt.

Lift from the grill and place around a large round platter.

To make dressing, whisk all ingredients together or blend in a processor or blender.

Mix the noodles, spring onions, carrots and capsicum with half the dressing. Tip onto the platter so that the noodles overlap some of the bok choy. Spoon the remaining dressing around and over the bok choy. Sprinkle with sesame seeds and serve immediately.

Vegetarian

ROASTED TOMATO AND RED ONION SOUP

→ INGREDIENTS

- 1 kg (35 oz) ripe tomatoes, hull removed and halved
- 150 g (5.3 oz) red onion, chopped
- 2 cloves garlic, roughly chopped
- ½ teaspoon white peppercorns
- ½ teaspoon caraway seeds
- 500 ml (17 fl oz) salt-reduced vegetable stock

→ METHOD

Preheat oven to 180ºC. Roast the tomatoes, onion and garlic for 30 minutes.

Puree the roasted items and pour into large saucepan – this will give you 1 litre (34 fl oz) of tomato puree.

Pound the peppercorns and caraway seeds to a fine powder and add to the puree. Pour in the stock and bring to a simmer. Continue cooking for 5 minutes and serve with good bread, or croutons instead of sliced bread. See Garlic Croutons recipe on page 17.

For a variation on this recipe, I have stirred in 1 tablespoon of fat-free evaporated milk to 400ml (13.5 fl oz) of soup – it lightens the colour and gives a touch of creaminess to it. This means you are serving the soup as a lunch item with two slices of good quality bread.

MIXED VEGETABLE STEW

SERVES 4

→ INGREDIENTS

- 160 g (5.7 oz) low-sodium, no-added-sugar tomatoes, crushed
- 240 ml (8 fl oz) low-sodium vegetable stock or water
- 200 g (7 oz) red capsicum (pepper), chopped
- 150 g (5.3 oz) red onion, chopped
- 125 g (4.4 oz) peeled carrot, chopped
- 125 g (4.4 oz) celery, chopped
- 125 g (4.4 oz) mushrooms, chopped
- 10 g (0.3 oz) garlic, chopped
- 1 large red chilli, chopped with seeds in
- 1 tablespoon parsley, chopped
- 1 teaspoon coriander powder
- 1 teaspoon ground black pepper

→ METHOD

Bring the tomatoes and stock to the boil. Add the other ingredients except for the parsley, coriander and black pepper. Simmer for 25 minutes, stirring regularly.

Check to see whether the vegetables are cooked after 25 minutes. Add the parsley, coriander and black pepper. Cook for another 5–7 minutes and serve.

I use this stew in so many ways. It makes a great lunch and is delicious served as a gravy with barbecued lamb or beef. I have used it under grilled fish and on its own, with some wholemeal pasta. This versatile dish can be frozen in portions to suit your needs.

SWEET POTATO AND RICOTTA LAYERED STACK

MAKES 4 SERVES

→ INGREDIENTS

- 365 g (12.8 oz) sweet potato pieces, around 2 cm (0.8 in) square
- 2 tablespoons mustard seed oil or vegetable oil
- 1 teaspoon caraway seeds
- 300 g (10.5 oz) reduced fat ricotta
- 100 g (3.5 oz) low-fat natural yoghurt
- 1 tablespoon curry powder
- 4 whole slices mountain bread
- 150 g (5.3 oz) semi-roasted tomatoes, roughly chopped
- Mixed salad leaves
- Lemon juice
- Ground black pepper

→ METHOD

Pre-heat oven to 200ºC.

Rub the sweet potato with oil and brown in oven. Remove, sprinkle with caraway seeds and let cool.

Mix the ricotta, yoghurt and curry powder well.

Line a baking tray with baking paper. Spread each piece of bread with ricotta mix. Put one in the bottom of the tray. Layer the ingredients in this order: sweet potato, bread slice, tomatoes, bread slice, sweet potato and top with last bread slice inverted to give a clean top to the stack. Lightly press, cover with cling wrap and refrigerate for 1 hour.

To serve, invert the stack onto a cutting board; cut in half to form two smaller rectangles or cut into quarters. Serve on individual plates with lemon doused salad leaves and sprinkle with ground black pepper.

Vegetarian

BUCKWHEAT PANCAKES AND CAPONATA

SERVES 4

→ INGREDIENTS

FOR THE CAPONATA

- 240ml (8 fl oz) low sodium vegetable stock
- 1 large onion, peeled and diced roughly
- 2 medium eggplants (aubergines), diced into 3cm (1.2 in) pieces
- 130 g (4.5 oz) diced celery
- 60 g (2 oz) green olives, chopped
- 325 g (11.5 oz) tomatoes, diced
- 40 g (1.3 oz) drained capers
- 60 ml (2 fl oz) lemon juice and zest of that lemon
- 1 tablespoon honey
- 2 bay leaves
- Basil leaves for garnish
- 8–12 pancakes

→ METHOD

Prepare the pancake batter first. Leave to sit for one hour before use.

Preheat oven to 180ºC. Put all the caponata ingredients into a casserole dish and cook in the oven for 1 hour. Stir occasionally, when done cool and refrigerate if not using immediately. The mixture needs to be dryish for this recipe. If you have too much juice, either spoon some out or simmer on top of the stove to reduce liquid.

Make and cook the pancakes as per recipe and keep warm.

To serve, lay out the pancakes and spoon the caponata down the centre. Roll the pancakes around the caponata filling and place on plates. This is best done with warm caponata, reheated in the microwave. Decorate with ripped basil leaves.

These are just great at room temperature too. If you want to slightly heat them, put them into a hot oven for 5 minutes and they are ready to eat.

The caponata freezes well, if you have any left over, or can be refrigerated for 7 days.

TOFU, CARROT AND LENTIL STRUDEL

→ INGREDIENTS

- 200 g (7 oz) carrots, peeled and grated
- 150 g (5.3 oz) firm tofu, diced
- 150 g (5.3 oz) precooked canned lentils, drained
- 10 pitted prunes
- 4 sheets filo pastry
- Spray canola oil
- 240 ml (8 fl oz) low-fat natural yoghurt
- 2 tablespoons fresh mint, chopped
- 1 teaspoon ground black pepper

→ METHOD

Preheat oven 180°C. Combine the carrots, tofu and lentils and mix well.

Lay one sheet of pastry on the bench and spray lightly with oil. Top with another sheet and repeat until the pastry is all used.

Spoon the carrot filling down one side of the assembled pastry layers. Dot with prunes, roll and pull in the ends to make a sealed package. Lift onto a baking paper-lined baking tray, spray with a light coating of oil and bake until browned and crisp, about 30–40 minutes.

Vegetarian

SALADS

CHARGRILLED VEGETABLES & PASTA SALAD WITH TOMATO BASIL DRESSING

SERVES 4

→ INGREDIENTS

- 2 small zucchinis (courgettes), trimmed and cut in half lengthwise
- 2 small carrots, peeled and cut in half lengthwise
- Spray vegetable oil
- 1 onion, coarsely chopped
- 230 g (8 oz) cauliflower flowerettes, blanched
- 8 tear drop tomatoes, halved
- 160 g (5.6 oz) tomato flesh, peeled and seeds removed
- 60 ml (2 fl oz) olive oil
- 10 basil leaves, ripped
- 1 teaspoon green peppercorns, rinsed
- Salt to taste
- 235 g (8.3 oz) spirali pasta, dry

→ METHOD

Spray zucchinis and carrots with vegetable oil and cook on a medium-hot grill until just cooked. Insert a skewer into them when soft but firm, then lift and cool. Spray onion with oil and cook on medium grill for 1 minute.

Put the cauliflower, onion and tear drop tomatoes into a salad bowl. Cut the carrot and zucchini into bite-sized pieces and add to the pasta mix.

Make the tomato dressing by blending the tomato flesh, oil, basil, peppercorns and salt in a blender or processor. When pureed, pour over the pasta and toss well to combine flavours.

Cook the pasta in plenty of boiling water until done – around 6–7 minutes. Strain and rinse under cold water. Drain well and tip into the vegetable mix while still hot. Add the dressing and mix well.

For the best combination of flavours, prepare this salad 4–5 hours before use and toss hourly.

BACON, PEACH & BLUE CHEESE SALAD
SERVES 4

→ INGREDIENTS

- 4 medium bacon rashers
- 2 firm peaches
- Juice of 1 small lemon
- 100 g (4 oz) mixed lettuce leaves
- 1 small radicchio, core removed, washed, dried and chilled
- 1 yellow capsicum (pepper), cut in strips
- 1 small red onion, in rings
- 100 g (4 oz) creamy blue vein cheese
- 2 tablespoons white balsamic vinegar
- Ground black pepper to taste
- 2 tablespoons chopped chives

→ METHOD

Cut the rind from the bacon and then cut into 3 cm (1.2 in) lengths cooked on hot plate until crisp. Drain on kitchen towel.

Slice the peaches into wedges. Toss in the juice of the lemon.

Mash the cheese with the vinegar – leave quite lumpy.

Assemble the salad by layering various leaves, capsicum, onion, peaches and bacon into a salad bowl. Spoon over the cheese dressing and sprinkle over the chopped chives. Serve immediately.

PEACH, FETA & PROSCIUTTO SALAD WITH LIME & LYCHEE DRESSING
SERVES 4

→ INGREDIENTS

- 24 peach slices, fresh and cut from the stone or canned and drained
- Spray oil
- 100 g (4 oz) mixed lettuce leaves
- 200 g (7 oz) feta cheese, diced
- 1 tablespoon extra virgin olive oil
- 3 tablespoons fresh lime juice
- 60 g (2 oz) lychee flesh, in 1 cm (½ in) dices (canned and drained)
- 1 teaspoon dill, chopped
- 1 teaspoon green peppercorns, crushed
- 4 large slices prosciutto, grilled on the barbecue to crisp, cooled and crumbled

→ METHOD

Lightly spray the peach slices with oil and lightly brown them on a hot grill; the canned slices cook very quickly while the fresh ones take a little longer. Do 6 slices at a time to have better control. Leave to cool before adding to the leaves and cheese.

Make the dressing by whisking the oil for a few seconds. Whisk in lime juice slowly and stir in the lychee dices, dill and pepper.

Pour the dressing onto the peach and salad ingredients and toss gently. Sprinkle crumbled prosciutto over and serve.

CHARGRILLED HALOUMI, CARROT & CHIVE SALAD
SERVES 4

→ INGREDIENTS

- 300 g (11 oz) carrots, peeled, halved lengthwise
- 120 ml (4 fl oz) orange juice
- 60 ml (2 fl oz) walnut oil
- ½ teaspoon powdered cumin
- ½ teaspoon powdered smoky paprika
- ¼ teaspoon powdered chilli
- Salt to taste
- 25 g (0.9 oz) garlic chives, in 4 cm (2 in) long pieces
- 4 x 2 cm (1 in) thick haloumi slices
- Spray olive oil

→ METHOD

Cut the halved carrots into half-moon shapes on the diagonal and boil for 2 minutes. Drain and keep warm.

Whisk the orange juice with oil, cumin, paprika, chilli and salt. Add the carrots and chives and toss well. Tip into salad bowl.

Spray the haloumi with a little oil, then cook on medium grill until lightly browned each side. Spread around the top of the carrots and serve while warm.

PUMPKIN, TOFU & PINK GRAPEFRUIT SALAD
SERVES 4

→ INGREDIENTS

- 300 g (11 oz) Japanese pumpkin, skin on and cut into bite size pieces
- Spray olive oil
- 200 g (7 oz) firm tofu, drained and cut into pieces around the same size as the pumpkin
- 2 pink grapefruit
- 120 ml (4 fl oz) olive oil
- ½ teaspoon honey
- ¼ teaspoon smoky paprika
- Sea salt and ground black pepper to taste
- 100 g (4 oz) baby rocket leaves

→ METHOD

Spray the pumpkin with oil and cook on medium-hot plate with the hood down or covered with large bowl, until done. Do the same with the tofu and cook on the flat plate as well.

Remove all the skin from the grapefruit on a plate so you capture all juices. Cut the segments out of the membrane over a bowl so you capture those juices too and put the segments into a separate bowl.

Take the pumpkin and tofu from the barbecue and cool on kitchen paper.

Whisk the grapefruit juice, oil, honey, paprika, salt and pepper together. It is good to have at least twice as much juice as oil. Put the pumpkin and tofu into the salad bowl and pour the grapefruit dressing over the cooling pumpkin and tofu and gently toss with your hands.

Allow to sit for 20 minutes.

When ready to serve, put the leaves in with the pumpkin and tofu, toss to coat leaves and mix. Clean down the inside of the bowl, spoon over the grapefruit segments and serve.

ZUCCHINI, HALOUMI & MUSHROOM OIL SALAD
SERVES 4

The haloumi needs to be served warm as it can toughen if left to cool too much.

→ INGREDIENTS

- 4 medium zucchinis (courgettes)
- 4 x 1 cm (½ in) thick slices haloumi cheese
- 100 g (4 oz) mixed lettuce leaves
- 1 tablespoon lemon juice
- 1 tablespoon mushroom oil (see recipe below)
- Spray oil

MUSHROOM OIL
- 200 g (7 oz) mushroom caps
- 250 g (9 oz) light olive oil

→ METHOD

Trim and cut the zucchinis in half lengthwise, sprinkle with a little salt, spray both sides with oil and cook on a hot grill until softened and marked. Start with cut side down and cook on both sides.

Spray the plate with oil and add the haloumi. Cook for 1 minute on each side.

Lift the zucchini and haloumi onto a kitchen towel lined plate and keep warm.

Pile equal quantities of leaves into the centre of individual plates. Top with the equal amounts of haloumi and zucchini and sprinkle over the lemon juice. Spoon the mushroom oil over the combined ingredients and serve.

FOR THE MUSHROOM OIL

Slice the mushrooms into pieces around 5 mm (¼ in) thick.

Spray a medium hot plate with oil and cook the mushrooms for 3 minutes without adding more oil. Lift mushrooms into an airtight storage container and pour the olive oil onto the mushrooms. Stir, close and keep in a cupboard for two days (do shake regularly or stir) before use and then use as soon as possible.

NECTARINE, PANCETTA & FETA SALAD WITH CINNAMON ZUCCHINI BREAD

SERVES 4

→ INGREDIENTS

- 2 large just ripe nectarines
- Spray oil
- 8 slices pancetta
- 200 g (7 oz) feta cheese, crumbled
- 100 g (4oz) mixed salad greens

- 120 ml (4 fl oz) olive oil
- 1 teaspoon Dijon mustard
- 2 tablespoons balsamic vinegar
- 8 slices cinnamon zucchini (courgette) bread (see recipe below)

→ METHOD

Wash the nectarines and halve, then cut the halves into wedges. Spray the wedges well with oil and mark on a hot grill. The wedges will cook quickly so turn regularly and remove when well marked.

Cook the pancetta at the same time on a hot plate. When crisped and browned, lift onto a plate lined with kitchen towel.

Make the dressing by whisking the oil and mustard in a bowl. When combined (the mixture looks as though it has curdled), whisk in the balsamic vinegar and set to one side but do not refrigerate.

Spray the bread and brown both sides on a medium hot grill.

Place the salad greens into a large bowl, top with the room temperature nectarine wedges, feta cheese, crumble the crispy pancetta over the salad and dress. Serve, in the middle of the table with the bread alongside.

Continued over page

NECTARINE, PANCETTA & FETA SALAD WITH CINNAMON ZUCCHINI BREAD, CONTINUED

→ INGREDIENTS

CINNAMON ZUCCHINI BREAD

- 375 g (13 oz) small zucchinis (courgettes), washed, trimmed and grated
- 1 egg beaten with 2 egg whites and 1 tablespoon olive oil
- 1 tablespoon honey

- 1 teaspoon ground cinnamon
- 400 g (14 oz) self raising wholemeal flour
- 1 teaspoon baking powder
- 60 g (2 oz) walnuts, crumbled
- Spray olive oil

→ METHOD

FOR THE CINNAMON ZUCCHINI BREAD

Preheat oven to 170°C.

Mix the zucchinis, eggs and oil, honey and cinnamon, stirring to combine well.

Fold in the flour and walnuts and leave to sit for 5 minutes.

Spray two bread tins 21cm long x 11cm wide and 6cm deep (8 x 4 x 2in) with olive oil. Spoon equal amounts of the zucchini mixture into the tins and cook in the oven for 1 hour or until a skewer comes out clean.

Leave in tin for 10 minutes to cool and turn onto a cooking rack to cool before slicing.

The zucchini keeps the bread moist during the cooking.

Makes 2 loaves.

THAI KANGAROO SALAD
SERVES 4

→ INGREDIENTS

- 400 g (14 oz) kangaroo strip loins
- 1 clove garlic, peeled
- 1 trimmed coriander root, washed and chopped
- 1 medium-hot green chilli, roughly chopped
- 1 lime, juiced
- 1 teaspoon fish sauce
- 2 teaspoons palm sugar (or brown sugar)

- 100 g (4 oz) mixed Asian lettuce leaves or similar
- 1 small Lebanese cucumber, washed and roughly diced
- 100 g (3.5 oz) snow pea shoots
- 4 tablespoons chopped coriander
- 50 g (1.8 oz) tightly packed fresh mint leaves
- Spray oil

→ METHOD

Trim the meat of all sinew and refrigerate until ready to use.

Make a paste with the garlic, coriander root, chilli, juice, fish sauce and sugar in a food processor or in a mortar and pestle. Tip into a flattish dish.

Remove the kangaroo from the refrigerator 10 minutes before use, spray the kangaroo with oil and sear on a hot plate. Cook for a couple of minutes only as the meat must be served rare. When done, remove from heat and let sit for 5 minutes to set juices.

Put the lettuce leaves, cucumber and pea shoots into a large mixing bowl. Slice the cooked meat and toss in the garlic coriander root mix to coat it and then put in with the lettuce. Rip the coriander and mint leaves and add the meat.

Toss the salad gently and then serve on a large platter or individual plates.

CUMIN PUMPKIN, YELLOW SQUASH & RED ONION SALAD
SERVES 4

→ INGREDIENTS

- 60 ml (2 fl oz) olive oil
- 1 tablespoon ground cumin
- ½ tablespoon ground rosemary
- ½ teaspoon ground white pepper
- 400 g (14 oz) butter nut pumpkin, peeled and cut into 2 cm (0.8 in) dices
- 200 g (7 oz) yellow squash, trimmed and cut into 2 cm (0.8 in) dices

- 1 medium red onion, skin and roots on and cut into 8 wedges
- 8 toothpicks
- Spray olive oil
- 2 tablespoons extra virgin olive oil
- 1 tablespoon balsamic vinegar
- 25 g (0.9 oz) baby watercress sprigs

→ METHOD

Mix the oil, cumin, rosemary and pepper in a large bowl. Add the pumpkin and squash and toss to coat the pieces. Let rest for 20 minutes.

Put a toothpick through the onion wedges lengthwise to hold them in place when cooking Leaving the root on also helps here.

Spoon the pumpkin mix onto a medium-hot plate and cook, turning often, for around 5–7 minutes or until softened and browned.

Spray the onion wedges and cook on the same plate for 5 minutes. The wedges need to be cooked but still holding their structure. Lift from the heat and cool. Peel the skin away, remove the toothpick and cut the root off.

Drain the pumpkin mix on kitchen towel and tip into a large bowl. Add the onions, oil and balsamic vinegar. Tumble to coat and mix flavours. Let cool before serving. Decorate with watercress.

KING PRAWN CAESAR SALAD
SERVES 4

→ INGREDIENTS

FOR THE SALAD

- 120 g (4 oz) cos lettuce, inner whitish leaves, washed, crisped and cut into bite-sized pieces
- 2 hard-boiled eggs, shelled and roughly chopped
- 4 tablespoons crisp bacon bits
- 50 g (1.7 oz) shaved parmesan cheese
- Garlic croutons to taste
- 24 medium green king prawns, peeled, deveined and with tail on and butterflied
- Spray oil

FOR THE DRESSING

- 3 anchovy fillets, well drained of oil
- 2 egg yolks
- 2 large cloves garlic, minced
- 1 teaspoon Worcestershire sauce
- 1 tablespoon white vinegar
- 120 ml (4 fl oz) olive oil

GARLIC CROUTONS

- 4 slices day-old sourdough bread
- 1 tablespoon garlic, crushed and mixed with 2 tablespoons olive oil

→ METHOD

Make the dressing in the bowl you will serve the salad in by mashing the anchovies with the back of a fork. Add the egg yolks, garlic, Worcestershire sauce and vinegar – combine until lighter in colour and thickening. Whisk in the oil slowly to make a thickish dressing.

Spray the prawns with oil and cook on medium-hot flat plate – toss to cook through; remove and keep at room temperature.

Add the cos lettuce, eggs, bacon and prawns to the dressing and toss to coat – sprinkle on the cheese and croutons.

Serve in the middle of table.

FOR THE GARLIC CROUTONS

Cut the bread into 2cm (1in) squares. Heat the garlic oil to medium-hot in a pan. Toss in the bread cubes and coat with the oil mixture. Cook on the wok burner until browned, turning regularly.

Tip onto a plate lined with kitchen paper when done.

CHERMOULA RUB ATLANTIC SALMON SALAD

→ INGREDIENTS

- 500 g (17.5 oz) Atlantic salmon fillet, skin removed and cut into strips 3 cm (1 in) wide
- Chermoula (see recipe below)
- 300 g (11 oz) Lebanese cucumber, deseeded
- 1 teaspoon salt
- 1 teaspoon sugar
- 60 ml (2 fl oz) white vinegar
- 2 tablespoons fennel seeds, crushed
- 100 g (4 oz) mixed lettuce leaves
- 8 asparagus spears, trimmed
- Spray oil

MY CHERMOULA

- 1 small onion, very finely chopped
- 2 teaspoons fresh coriander leaves, finely chopped
- 4 teaspoons parsley, finely chopped
- 2 cloves garlic, minced
- 1 small red chilli, finely chopped
- 4 teaspoons ground cumin seeds
- 2 teaspoons mild paprika
- 1 teaspoon powdered tumeric
- ¼ teaspoon cayenne pepper
- 4 tablespoons olive oil
- ¼ teaspoon salt
- ¼ teaspoon ground black pepper

→ METHOD

FOR THE CHERMOULA

Mix all the ingredients together in a bowl or you can process them into a paste if you prefer.

Pat the salmon strips with the Chermoula and let sit for 10 minutes.

Using a vegetable peeler, cut the cucumber into longish ribbons and put into a bowl. Add the salt, sugar, vinegar and fennel. Stir, cover and refrigerate for 1 hour.

Lift the salmon strips from the Chermoula, shake off excess and spray well with oil. Cook on hot plate until medium, turning often. Remove from the plate when done and cool.

Spray the asparagus and cook on a hot grill for 2–3 minutes. Remove, cool and cut into bite-sized pieces.

Place the mixed leaves onto a large platter and scatter the cucumber strips across the top of the leaves. Break/flake the fish onto the leaves and sprinkle cucumber liquid over the top. Serve with good bread.

PORK, GREEN APPLE & VERMICELLI NOODLE SALAD
`SERVES 4`

→ INGREDIENTS

- 400 g (14 oz) pork fillet, in one piece
- Spray oil
- 2 medium green apples or mangoes
- ½ teaspoon salt
- 1 tablespoon vegetable oil
- 2 cloves garlic, sliced
- 4 green spring onions, trimmed and sliced diagonally
- 1 tablespoon fish sauce
- 1 teaspoon palm sugar, finely grated
- 1 tablespoon lime juice
- ½ teaspoon ground white pepper
- 1 large green chilli, deseeded and finely sliced
- 90 g (3.2 oz) vermicelli noodles, rehydrated
- 2 tablespoons roasted peanuts, crushed

→ METHOD

Trim the pork to make sure all fat and silver tissue is removed.

If using mangoes, peel and slice from the seed – slice very finely into half-moon shapes. Place the mango or apple slices into a bowl and sprinkle with salt. Pour in oil and toss. Add the garlic and spring onions. Mix the fish sauce, sugar, lime juice and pepper and pour onto the mango/apple ingredients. Tip in the chilli and noodles and toss well.

Spray the pork fillet with oil and seal on a hot plate by rolling it around. When browned all over, lower the hood to cook to medium-to-well done. Do not overcook the pork fillet and remove to rest for 10 minutes.

Slice the pork finely into rounds and halve if large slices. Add to the mango/apple salad and toss gently. Serve heaped into the centre of individual bowls and sprinkled with the crushed peanuts.

SWEET POTATO LAYER CAKE AND LENTIL SALAD
SERVES 4

→ INGREDIENTS

- Spray olive oil
- 200 g (7 oz) pumpkin, peeled, finely sliced
- 300 g (10.5 oz) Desiree potatoes, skin on, finely sliced
- 200 g (7 oz) sweet potato, peeled, finely sliced
- ½ teaspoon nutmeg, ground
- 60 ml (2 fl oz) salt-reduced chicken stock
- 400 g (14 oz) green lentils, cooked, drained
- 2 tablespoons spring onion, finely chopped
- 3 tablespoons oil-free vinaigrette
- 2 tablespoons oregano sprigs, chopped
- 100 g (3.5 oz) mixed lettuce

→ METHOD

Preheat oven to 180ºC. Spray a loaf tin with a film of oil. Line the bottom of tin with baking paper – spray that with oil too.

For colour, the potato is a good break between the orange colours. Start with a layer of pumpkin, then potato, then sweet potato and finish with a layer of potato. Sprinkle with nutmeg as you go – pour over the stock, top with a piece of sprayed baking paper and bake for 75 minutes. You can put a layer of weights that you would use for blind baking (rice/dried beans) on top of the baking paper. This way the cake is pressed as it cooks.

Remove from oven and cool for 5 minutes; leave weight on as it cools and refrigerate.

Combine the lentils, spring onions, vinaigrette and oregano for the salad. Toss well and keep refrigerated until ready to serve.

Slice down the loaf to serve – it makes around 800 g (28 oz) so there is plenty for a meatless meal. Add small lettuce leaves to the side of each plate and spoon the lentil salad over the top of them. I serve this with a wedge of lemon.

This layer cake is best cooked the day before so the vegetables stick together when you slice it.

GLASS NOODLE SALAD
SERVES 4

→ INGREDIENTS

- 125 g (4.5 oz) dried bean thread noodles
- 100 g (3.5 oz) daikon (Japanese white radish), peeled and finely shredded
- ½ telegraph cucumber, cut lengthwise and then into half moons
- 1 very small Spanish onion, peeled and sliced very finely
- 50 g (1.7 oz) Japanese pickled ginger, finely sliced
- 50 g (1.7 oz) snow pea sprouts, washed and crisped
- Coriander leaves for decoration (optional)

DRESSING

- 1 tablespoon palm sugar
- 100 ml (3.4 fl oz) coconut cream
- 2 limes, juiced
- 1–2 tablespoons fish sauce (nam pla)

→ METHOD

Put the noodles into a large bowl and pour boiling water over to cover them – let sit for 5–10 minutes and then strain. Run under cold water to stop cooking. Ensure all the water is removed and tip the noodles into a mixing bowl and allow to cool for 10 minutes.

Add all the other ingredients except for the coriander leaves and toss gently using your hands.

Make the dressing by combining all the ingredients and mixing well. Pour over the assembled salad ingredients and toss gently. Top with the coriander leaves and serve as a side salad.

CUMIN-INFUSED PUMPKIN, ZUCCHINI AND SPANISH ONION SALAD

SERVES 4

→ INGREDIENTS

- 60 ml (2 fl oz) olive oil
- 1 tablespoon cumin, ground
- ½ tablespoon rosemary, ground
- ½ teaspoon white pepper, ground
- 400 g (14 oz) butternut pumpkin, peeled and cut into 2 cm (0.8 in) dices
- 200 g (7 oz) zucchini (courgette), trimmed and cut into 2 cm (0.8 in) dices

- 1 medium Spanish onion, skin and roots on, cut into 8 wedges
- 8 toothpicks
- Olive oil spray
- 2 tablespoons extra virgin olive oil
- 1 tablespoon balsamic vinegar
- 25 g (0.9 oz) baby watercress sprigs

→ METHOD

Mix the oil, cumin, rosemary and pepper in a large bowl. Add the pumpkin and zucchini and toss to coat the pieces. Marinate for 20 minutes.

Spoon the pumpkin mix onto a medium–hot flat plate and turn and cook for around 5–10 minutes or until soft and browned. Spray the onion wedges and cook on the same plate for 5 minutes – they need to be cooked but still holding their structure. Remove from the heat and cool. Peel the skin away, remove the toothpicks and cut the roots off.

Drain the pumpkin mix on absorbent paper and tip into a large bowl. Add the onions, rosemary, oil and balsamic vinegar. Tumble to coat and mix flavours and let cool before serving. Decorate with the watercress and serve.

Put a toothpick lengthwise through the onion wedges to hold them in place when cooking— leaving the root on also helps.

BARBECUED POTATO SALAD WITH ANCHOVY AND GARLIC DRESSING
SERVES 4

→ INGREDIENTS

- 400 g (14 oz) Kipfler potatoes (Pink Fir Apple or baby Desiree will do too)
- Olive oil spray
- 3 green spring onions, white only and finely sliced
- 2 hard-boiled eggs, shells removed and roughly chopped
- 2 tablespoons crisp bacon pieces
- 3 tablespoons mint, roughly chopped
- 4 anchovy fillets, drained well
- 4 cloves garlic, poached for 5 minutes
- 120 ml (4 fl oz) good mayonnaise
- 60 ml (2 fl oz) white vinegar
- ½ teaspoon ground black pepper

→ METHOD

Cut the potatoes on the diagonal into bite-sized pieces. Boil in salted water for 5 minutes – drain well and cool. When cool enough to handle, spray with oil and cook until tender on a medium–hot open grill.

Remove from the barbecue and tip into large mixing bowl. Add the spring onions, eggs, bacon and mint.

Mash the anchovies with the garlic. Stir in the mayonnaise, vinegar and ground black pepper to taste and pour over the potato mixture.

Toss to coat the ingredients and leave to cool. Refrigerate to use when needed.

This salad is made when the potatoes are warm and the day before use.

SWEET POTATO WITH TUNA DRESSING
SERVES 4

→ INGREDIENTS

SALAD

- 600 g (21 oz) whole sweet potatoes
- Oil spray
- 100 g (3.5 oz) Spanish onion, finely chopped
- 150 g (5.4 oz) celery, finely diced
- 25 g (0.9 oz) mustard cress leaves,

DRESSING

- 180 g (6.3 oz) canned tuna, drained
- 335 ml (11.8 fl oz) mayonnaise
- 1 tablespoon white vinegar
- ½ teaspoon sea salt
- ¼ teaspoon white pepper

→ METHOD

Prick the sweet potato all over with a dinner fork and cook in the microwave, on high, for 3 minutes. Remove and cool. Cut into 2 cm (0.8 in)-thick rounds, spray the flat surfaces with oil and cook on a medium–hot flat plate for 2 minutes each side. If you like, you can crisp them on the open grill, but be careful because they caramelise very quickly. Remove and cool on absorbent paper.

Make the dressing by blending or processing all ingredients to a smooth, creamy consistency.

Spread the sweet potato slices around a flat plate so they overlap. Spoon dressing over the top, sprinkle with the onion, celery and cress and serve.

DESSERT

PASSIONFRUIT SOUFFLE
SERVES 4

Make sure you have plenty of room on the rack for the soufflé dishes (or tea cups in my case) so you can move them. You can open the lid and move the soufflés very gently if they are not getting even heat and are tending to look lopsided. Through experience, I have found the tops will brown very quickly if the sugar is not incorporated into the egg whites properly.

→ INGREDIENTS

- 30g (1oz) butter, melted
- 1 tablespoon castor sugar
- 3 egg whites, at room temperature
- 65 g (2.2 oz) castor sugar for the egg
- whites
- 170 g (6 oz) passionfruit in syrup
- Icing sugar
- Vanilla ice-cream or whipped cream

→ METHOD

Preheat barbecue to 180°C.

Brush four 250 ml (8 fl oz) ovenproof dishes or teacups with butter to lightly grease. Sprinkle with the sugar, shaking off any excess and refrigerate for 5 minutes.

Beat egg whites with an electric beater in a large, clean bowl until soft peaks form. Sprinkle in the extra castor sugar slowly, so it may dissolve and become incorporated into the egg whites.

It is important that the sugar be dissolved into the whites. You do not need really firm peaks in the beaten whites.

Fold passionfruit into egg whites using a sharp-sided metal spoon. Gently spoon the mixture into the cups and use a flat edge spatula to smooth the tops.

Run a thumb around inside rim of dishes or cups and place on a baking tray.

Sit on the dishes on a baking tray, and place on a cake cooling rack (for ease of handling) in the centre of the barbecue, not over direct heat. Cook for 8–10 minutes or until risen.

Dust with icing sugar and serve immediately with ice-cream or cream on the side.

SAMBUCCA MANGO CHEEKS & MINTED CRÈME FRAICHE

SERVES 4

→ INGREDIENTS

- 4 medium ripe mangoes
- 1 tablespoon icing sugar
- 240 ml (8 fl oz) crème fraiche
- 2 tablespoons honey
- 2 tablespoons ripped mint leaves (spearmint if possible)
- 120 ml (4 fl oz) white Sambucca

→ METHOD

Mix the crème fraiche with the honey and mint leaves at least 3 hours before use. Refrigerate until ready to serve.

Cut the cheeks from the mangoes and cut diamond shapes into the cheek without cutting through the skin.

Sprinkle the cut sides of the mango cheeks with equal amounts of the icing sugar and leave to sit until the sugar melts. Put the cheeks onto a clean hot grill to cook for a minute or so. The cheeks will brown very quickly, so turn them gently, as you want to retain the marks of the grill. Leave the cheeks, skin-side down, for 30 seconds and remove.

Serve the two cheeks on individual plates, sprinkle with Sambucca and add the crème fraiche to one side.

BANANAS, RUM & WHIPPED MASCARPONE
SERVES 4

You can buy vanilla sugar at the supermarket, but it is so easy to make. I always have my castor sugar with a whole vanilla pod stuck in it. You can use a vanilla bean to infuse milk for custards. After the milk has been infused, remove the bean from the milk, wash it and dry it, then return it to the castor sugar.

→ INGREDIENTS
- 200 ml (7 fl oz) mascarpone
- 50 ml (2 fl oz) pouring cream
- 2 tablespoons vanilla sugar
- 8 lady finger bananas, peeled, not too ripe
- 2 tablespoon butter, melted
- 60 ml (2 fl oz) rum

→ METHOD
Whip the mascarpone with the cream and the vanilla sugar.

Place bananas onto a low-heat plate and spoon over the melted butter. Turn the bananas gently using a long spatula and a set of tongs. Cook for four minutes and lift onto a serving plate.

Pour the rum over the bananas and serve with the whipped mascarpone spooned over as you serve.

Dessert

CINNAMON FRENCH TOAST & COINTREAU CREAM

`SERVES 4`

→ INGREDIENTS

- 4 x 1.5 cm (½ in) thick slices raisin bread or good fruit bread
- 3 eggs, lightly beaten
- 240 ml (8 fl oz) milk
- 1 teaspoon powdered cinnamon
- 200 ml (7 fl oz) pouring cream, stiffly beaten
- 60 ml (2 fl oz) Cointreau
- 2 tablespoons butter, melted
- Icing sugar

→ METHOD

Cut the crusts from the bread if you like. Combine the eggs, milk and cinnamon.

Mix the whipped cream and Cointreau together and refrigerate.

To cook, dip the raisin toast in the egg mixture and place onto a hot, lightly oiled plate. Cook for one minute and turn onto a lightly oiled part of the plate that has not been used. Cook for 1–2 minutes and lift from the plate onto individual plates and spoon over the melted butter and dredge with icing sugar.

Serve a slice of this special French toast with a really good dollop of the Cointreau cream.

You can serve almost any stewed fruit with this raisin toast, but one of my personal favourites is stewed rhubarb and apple which has a lovely bite to it to counteract the sugar rush in this dessert.

POLENTA GRIDDLE CAKES, BANANA & CARAMEL SAUCE
SERVES 4

→ INGREDIENTS

FOR THE CAKES
- 56g (2 oz) plain flour
- 100 g (3.5 oz) yellow polenta
- 1 teaspoon salt
- ½ teaspoon bicarbonate of soda
- 1 teaspoon baking powder
- 28 g (1 oz) self-raising flour
- 2 tablespoons butter, melted
- 240 ml (8 fl oz) milk
- 1 egg, beaten
- 4 medium bananas
- Icing sugar for dusting

FOR THE CARAMEL SAUCE
- 200 g (7 oz) brown (soft) sugar
- 300 ml (10 fl oz) pouring cream
- Spray oil
- Extra butter

→ METHOD

Mix the flour, polenta, salt, bicarbonate of soda, baking powder and self-raising flour together in a bowl. Make a well and stir in the well combined butter, milk and egg. Stir well and use immediately, as the polenta soaks up the liquid very quickly. If the batter gets too thick at the barbecue, add a little milk.

Spray a medium-hot plate well. Add a little butter and when foaming spread over the part of the plate to be used and spoon some of the cake mixture onto the plate. Make only 3 or 4 at a time and when browned on one side, flip over to cook the cakes through. Repeat until all the batter is used. If the batter thickens while waiting to be cooked, add a little more milk.

Make the caramel sauce by putting the sugar into a small saucepan and start to melt over medium heat. Remove from the heat and stir in the cream. Return to the heat and stir to combine.

Keep the cakes warm. Put a little butter in between each of the cakes and pile at least two-high. Slice peeled banana over the cakes and pour on some caramel sauce. Dust with icing sugar to serve.

Dessert

ORANGE AND HAZELNUT CAKE

→ INGREDIENTS

- 2 medium oranges, raw weight 400 g (14 oz)
- 1 cinnamon curl
- 250 g (8.8 oz) hazelnut meal
- 4 eggs white and 2 whole eggs
- 120 g (4.2 oz) spelt flour
- 45 g (1.5 oz) yellow polenta
- 60 ml (2 fl oz) honey, warmed (in microwave) for easy pouring
- 1 teaspoon baking powder
- 1 teaspoon nutmeg, grated
- 2 oranges cut into skinless segments for garnish

→ METHOD

Cover the two oranges with water and bring to the boil. Break the cinnamon curl over the top, drop in, reduce to a simmer and cook for 60 minutes. When done, remove from the heat and lift out the oranges to cool. Keep the cooking liquid to use later or reduce to a syrup to spoon over the cake.

Line 2 x 21cm (8in) non-stick, round sponge cake tins with baking paper.

Preheat oven to 170ºC. Break the cooked oranges open, remove seeds and drop into the food processor bowl. Add the hazelnut meal, egg white and eggs.

Start the processor and feed the flour, polenta, honey, baking powder and nutmeg through the shute. When combined well, pour equal amounts into each of the tins. Cook at 170ºC for 45–60 minutes or until an inserted skewer comes out clean.

Let the cakes cool in their tins for 10 minutes and remove to cool further. Serve with the orange segments and a sprinkle of icing sugar (optional).

This is a solid cake that does not rise very much and, when cooling, will set well. It stores well for a week in an airtight container. You will get 10 good-sized wedges from these cakes.

Spelt is an excellent flour as it reacts well in cooking and has great fibre. The polenta gives a texture I like. You can use almond meal instead of hazelnuts.

APPLE, RHUBARB AND GINGER CRUMBLE
SERVES 6

This dessert comes from another book on Low GI recipes: The Low GI Vegetarian Cookbook.

→ INGREDIENTS

- 400 g (14 oz) (about 3 small) Granny Smith apples, peeled, cored and cut into thin wedges
- 1 small bunch (about 350 g (12.3 oz)) rhubarb, ends trimmed, washed, cut into 4cm (1.5 in) lengths
- 1 teaspoon ginger, finely grated
- 2 tablespoons caster sugar
- 1 cinnamon stick

FOR THE CRUMBLE
- 2 tablespoons plain flour
- 40 g (1.4 oz) almond meal
- 3 tablespoons reduced-fat margarine
- 50 g (1.7 oz) rolled oats
- 40 g (1.4 oz) natural almonds, roughly chopped
- 3 tablespoons brown sugar
- ½ teaspoon ground ginger

→ METHOD

Preheat the oven to 180°C. Lightly grease a 1.5-litre (50 fl oz) ovenproof dish.

Place the apples, rhubarb, ginger, sugar and cinnamon with 170 ml (5.7 fl oz) water in a medium-sized saucepan and simmer for 15 minutes, or until the apples and rhubarb are just cooked.

Meanwhile, for the crumble, place the flour and almond meal in a bowl. Use your fingertips to rub in the margarine until well combined and large crumbs form. Mix in the oats, almonds, sugar and ginger.

Spoon the fruit into the prepared dish and sprinkle the crumble over evenly. Bake for 20 minutes or until golden and bubbling. Set aside to cool for 5 minutes before serving.

This crumble can be made as four individual crumbles or as a whole. If rhubarb is not available you could substitute the rhubarb with more apple.

LOW-FAT PASSIONFRUIT FROZEN CUSTARD
SERVES 6

→ INGREDIENTS

- 250 g (8.8 oz) passionfruit pulp (I use canned)
- 240 ml (8 fl oz) water
- 2 tablespoons honey
- 450 ml (15 fl oz) low-fat pre-made custard
- 400 ml (13.5 fl oz) no-fat natural yoghurt

→ METHOD

Bring the passionfruit, water and honey to the boil. Simmer for at least 5 minutes, then cool.

Whisk the custard and yoghurt together well and fold in the cooled passionfruit. Freeze in a 20 cm (8 in) loaf tin for 2 hours.

Remove from freezer and spoon into food processor; work into a smooth paste, return to tin and freeze until solid and ready to use. If not using immediately, cover with cling wrap or a lid to prevent freezer flavours developing.

Serve in balls shaped with an ice-cream scoop.

I serve this when there are children around and they love it; given the amount of children now being stricken with type 2 diabetes, this dessert can become a staple sweet for you and your children.

BLUEBERRY CHEESECAKES
MAKES 4

This delicious dessert comes from The Low GI Diet by Prof. Jennie Brand-Miller, Kaye Foster-Powell and Joanna McMillan-Price. They are the specialists in this field of GI (Glycaemic Index) by which I now live my life.

→ INGREDIENTS

- 300 g (10.5 oz) low-fat ricotta
- 1 tablespoon honey
- 1 teaspoon orange rind, finely grated
- 150 g (5 oz) fresh blueberries
- 40 g (1.4 oz) walnuts, finely chopped
- 4 strawberries, sliced

→ METHOD

Line four half-cup-capacity ramekins with plastic wrap.

Place the ricotta, honey and orange rind in a bowl and mash with a fork.

Combine two-thirds of the blueberries with the ricotta mixture and divide between the ramekins. Press in firmly and smooth the surface.

Sprinkle over the walnuts. Smooth out with the back of a spoon and press the nuts into the mixture. Refrigerate for 1 hour, to firm and chill.

To serve, invert onto a plate and peel away the plastic wrap. Top each cake with a sliced strawberry, and serve with the remaining blueberries.

COCONUT CITRUS PUDDING
SERVES 8

→ INGREDIENTS

- 4 eggs
- 180 ml (6 fl oz) honey
- 60 ml (2 fl oz) vegetable oil
- 125 g (4.4 oz) almonds, chopped
- 70 g (2.5 oz) coconut, desiccated
- finely grated zest of 1 orange and 1 lemon
- 120 ml (4 fl oz) fresh orange juice
- 120 ml (4 fl oz) fresh lemon juice
- 120 ml (4 fl oz) skim milk
- 55 g (1.9 oz) plain flour, sifted with 1 teaspoon baking powder
- Spray canola oil

→ METHOD

Pre-heat oven to 180ºC. Put all ingredients into a food processor, except for the spray canola oil, and blend for at least 1 minute.

Pour into a deep pie dish that has been lightly sprayed with oil.

Cook for 30–40 minutes or until set and golden brown. Cool and serve with flavoured yoghurt of your choice.

This cooks in 30 minutes and I leave them to cool before easing them out of the bowl. I then slice the wedges to serve 8 and serve them with the yoghurt. This is a very intense pudding, dense but delicious.

I also make this using four individual pie dishes. I use Chinese bowls and divide the mixture evenly into the four lightly oiled containers.

INDEX